Reading this book had a p
was living each chapter in
having the experiences desc
were actually "clues" to pro
past years. You actually had
this book, for there is absolutely no other way you could have
written such a masterpiece! Congratulations on such a wonderful
accomplishment!

—RHONDA TARVER, FRIEND

The

SECRET PLACE

Constance Parks

**CREATION
HOUSE**

THE SECRET PLACE: THE GARDEN OF LOVE
by Constance Parks
Published by Creation House
A Charisma Media Company
600 Rinehart Road
Lake Mary, Florida 32746
www.charismamedia.com

Unless otherwise noted, all Scripture quotations are from the New King James Version of the Bible. Copyright © 1979, 1980, 1982 by Thomas Nelson, Inc., publishers. Used by permission.

Scripture quotations marked AMPC are from the Amplified Bible, Classic Edition. Old Testament copyright © 1965, 1987 by the Zondervan Corporation. The Amplified New Testament copyright © 1954, 1958, 1987 by the Lockman Foundation. Used by permission.

Scripture quotations marked NAS are from the New American Standard Bible–Updated Edition, Copyright © 1960, 1962, 1963, 1968, 1971, 1972, 1973, 1975, 1977, 1995 by The Lockman Foundation. Used by permission. (www.Lockman.org)

Scripture quotations marked NIV are from the Holy Bible, New International Version. Copyright © 1973, 1978, 1984, 2010, 2011, International Bible Society. Used by permission.

Scripture quotations marked NLT are from the Holy Bible, New Living Translation, copyright © 1996. Used by permission of Tyndale House Publishers, Inc., Wheaton, IL 60189. All rights reserved.

Design Director: Justin Evans
Cover design by Judith McKittrick Wright
Back cover photo: Nanaphotography by Wanda Kay

Visit the author's website: www.gardengatewayinternational.com.

Library of Congress Control Number: 2015952362
International Standard Book Number: 978-1-62998-498-8
E-book International Standard Book Number: 978-1-62998-499-5

While the author has made every effort to provide accurate telephone numbers and Internet addresses at the time of publication, neither the publisher nor the author assumes any responsibility for errors or for changes that occur after publication.

17 18 19 20 21 — 98765432
Printed in the United States of America

CONTENTS

THE SECRET PLACE:
THE GARDEN OF LOVE TEACHING AND STUDY GUIDE

ACKNOWLEDGMENTS

F IRST I WOULD like to thank Yeshua my Lord for His gift of love and His trust in allowing me to write this book. I thank my wonderful husband, Bruce, and my two sons, Michael and Andrew, for all the encouragement in the publishing of this book.

I would like to thank my three sets of spiritual parents: Pastor Richard and Tena Ford, who raised this child up in the way she should go; Pastor Curry and Beverly Juneau and Pastors Greg and Lenda Crawford, who allowed me to stretch and spread my wings to soar and enlarge my territory.

I would also like to thank my sisters, Randi Brewer and Robbie Tolson, who are not only my natural sisters but also my spiritual sisters who encouraged me and prayed me through this first book.

A special thanks to Jim Brooks for typing up and putting on disk the first manuscript, and also to all my friends for their encouragement.

Finally, to those who were so encouraging to me who have already gone to meet my Beloved in the heavenly sphere: my natural parents, John and Anita Lillard, who first instilled godly values in my life; and Annette Weathersbee, Annette Parks, and Pam Tarwater; I give God the praise for putting them in my life and I dedicate this book to them.

PREFACE

❧

THIS BOOK WAS written to encourage you to find the Lord Yeshua on a deeper level. You must put yourself into the pages of this book. Think of yourself as the beloved, for Yeshua wants to speak to you. He wants to heal you and make you whole. Yeshua can love you so fully like no one else can. It says in Jeremiah 31:3 that God (Yeshua) has loved us with an everlasting love and with lovingkindness He will draw us.

As you abandon yourself to this love of His, He will share with you His most intimate secrets, the mysteries of the universe, for He is the Master of the universe.

Therefore, this book is dedicated to those people, male or female, who are looking for love—that missing part of themselves. To those who have been called and chosen by the Master but who have not yet found Him, you will find what you are looking for in this book.

These scriptures have had a profound impact on my life:

> Let him kiss me with the kisses of his mouth—For your love is better than wine. Because of the fragrance of your good ointments, your name is ointment poured forth; Therefore the virgins love you.
> —SONG OF SOLOMON 1:2–3

> The Lord has appeared of old to me, saying, "Yes, I have loved you with an everlasting love. Therefore, with loving-kindness I have drawn you."
> —JEREMIAH 31:3

I drew them with gentle cords, With bands [ties] of love, And I was to them as those who takes the yoke from their neck. I stooped and fed them.

—HOSEA 11:4

"And you shall love the LORD your God with all your heart, with all your soul, with all your mind, and with all your strength." This is the first commandment.

—MARK 12:30

Behold, I stand at the door and knock. If anyone hears My voice and opens the door, I will come in to him and dine with him, and he with Me.

—REVELATION 3:20

Part 1

THE JOURNEY

⟲

CHAPTER 1

JUST FRIENDS

❧

MY LIFE HAS been such a struggle with so many things pulling here and pulling there. I can't seem to do the things that I know I should do. I feel so lost and empty inside. Guilt and shame surround me on all sides. There is no peace, no joy within me, no satisfaction in any thing I do. My life is such a mess and there is so much pain and rejection in my heart from things in my past. Is there any hope for someone like me? Is there anyone anywhere who can save me? How could anyone want anything to do with the ugly, miserable, and wretched person that I am? I go about my days doing things necessary to sustain life, but nothing has any meaning. I am like a prisoner in this world, chained to the everyday drudge of life. Where is true joy? Where is true peace? Where is true love?

When I see love, joy, or peace in others, it doesn't seem real. It's all fake, or just a put on, or it's the result of some external influence. Nothing meaningful ever seems to come into my life. There is no true peace that comes from within. Who can save me from this unending hurt? I don't even know if I want to live any longer. Who will deliver me from this prison of pain and rejection?

Then, one day it happened. I met Him, the one who would love me forever. His name is Yeshua Adonai, and He came into my life and has changed me forever.

Yeshua came into my life one grand and glorious, sunny day. He said to me,

> *I have been looking for you. I have searched the world over, and now I have found you. I have come to set you free from your prison and to remove your chains of bondage. If you will follow Me, I will set you free. I AM Yeshua. If you will*

believe in Me and put your unwavering trust in Me and
call on My name, Yeshua Adonai, your life will be changed
and you will never be the same.

Yeshua said to me,

With an everlasting love I love you, and with loving kind-
ness have I drawn you unto Myself. I have poured out My
very heart for you. My beloved, how I do love you! Every-
thing about you, just the way you are, is pleasing to Me.
Come with Me. Come away with Me into My kingdom.
Let me be your Prince of Peace and the love of your heart.
I have come calling your name, seeking your face, and
knocking upon the door of your heart. Open that door to
your heart and let me in, and I will come into your heart
to give you a new and meaningful life. The life I give you
is like streams of water flowing in the desert. And that life-
giving water will bring My living garden into the midst of
your heart.

Come, let us walk in the garden together. I delight in
spending time with you walking and talking together in the
cool of the day. You are precious to Me, and I rejoice being
in your presence. Come, follow Me, and I will put you on
the pathway to victory in every area of your life. Although
storms may rage all around, I have made you more than a
conqueror. I have made you an overcomer through all the
storms of life. I AM the one who is able to satisfy your
every need. For every desperate need you have, I will meet
that need because whosoever hungers and thirsts for the
truth and righteousness will be satisfied. So, My beloved,
come away with Me. You have need of so much love, and it
is only that which I give that can satisfy. Your heart is like
an empty well. I have come to bring the water of life and to
fill your well with the love that you need.

Everything about Yeshua Adonai was all I had been looking for.
True peace exuded out of Him. There was such a glow, such an
overwhelming radiance that came from within Him. All I could say

to Him was simply, "Yes!" Without even a thought, I just started speaking,

> *Yes, I do believe in You and I will put all my trust in You. I do choose to call on Your name, Yeshua. I repent, O Prince of Peace and love of my heart, of all my sins. I choose to lean on You and to rely on You and to trust in Your strength, Your power, and Your abilities to change me and to give me new life. Yeshua, will You come and live in my heart?*

His word was comfort to me as He said,

> *I will live in your heart and provide you with everything you need. I will take care of you as a shepherd takes care of his sheep. I stand in My Father's authority to tell you that you are forgiven of your sins. Also I have come to take away all the guilt and the shame you have felt for doing things wrong and for having hurt other people, as well as all those other things you have been feeling guilty of when you committed sin. You have received My forgiveness. There is therefore no condemnation for those who are in Me, who walk not after the flesh, but after the things the Spirit desires. I will take your guilt and shame away when you have confessed your sins and repented by turning away from them.*

Then He said,

> *My Spirit, the Holy Spirit, will always be with you. He will be your Counselor and your Helper, and He will magnify My presence to you, in you, and through you. He will also manifest in you grace, mercy, wisdom, and faith. Are you ready to receive My Spirit into your heart?*

I said to Him,

> *Yes! "Holy Spirit, come and live in my heart."*

Then He said,

> *Breathe deeply and receive My Spirit.*

I took a deep breath and received His Spirit. It was wonderful. I felt so warm inside and there was so much love flowing in me and through me and out of me. I could hardly stand up for all the power that was flowing all around my body. It was so glorious, so awesome, that words cannot seem to express just what I felt. I stood there only for a moment, yet it seemed as though I had been there for an eternity. He then assured me,

My Spirit will always be with you. He will never leave you.

And then He continued,

Now I want to tell you about My life. I grew up in a small town, the son of a carpenter. I was the eldest of My brothers and sisters. When My earthly father died, I was a young adult. I took over the business in which we built tables and chairs and yokes for oxen and other farming tools.

One evening My entire family went out to attend a wedding celebration. It so happened that they ran out of wine. My mother stood up and said to Me, "They have no wine." I replied to her, "Woman, it's not yet My time." She told the servants, "Whatever He tells you to do, you do it." There were six large empty water pots, so I told them, "Fill them all with water," and they did so, all the way to the brim. Then I said, "Now draw some out and take it to the ruler of the feast." And they did as I bid them. As the ruler of the feast tasted the water, it was turned into wine. He said, "The best, I believe, I have ever tasted."

All My life I knew I was born for a special purpose, and that My "earthly" father was not actually My real Father at all. My real Father is not of this world. Quite often I would spend hours talking to My real Father. Each time we talked He would reveal details of My purpose for being here. So that when this happened at the wedding feast, I did it because I had seen My Father do such things.

My real Father loves all people very much. Many, just like you, are prisoners and are bound to the god of this world and its system. My Father wants them all set free;

and He showed Me how they are to be set free. So that is just exactly what I would do. People who were sick in mind and body, as I touched them, they were healed and set free. But there were those in power who were jealous of what I was doing, and they hated Me. They hated Me so much that when the time came for Me to fulfill My purpose they came to take Me to kill Me.

Then Yeshua smiled and said,

I also had many friends, especially twelve men, with whom I spent many hours teaching what My Father taught Me. On one of those occasions, we were together at the house of one of the Pharisees. Then a woman, whom they declared a sinner, brought with her an alabaster box of ointment. She stood at My feet as we sat dining. Weeping she turned and knelt behind Me. As she wept she began to wash My feet with her tears and wipe My feet with the hair of her head. After she had kissed My feet, she anointed them with the ointment. She did this out of love and in preparation for My burial. I explained to and taught My friends that this act which she had done is not only pure intimacy, but also true worship.

The time came that I was to be offered up. So I sent My disciples before Me into a village of the Samaritans to make things ready for Me. But they did not receive us, or the Father's message, because I was set to go to Yerusalem instead of remaining there with them. Of the twelve men, James and John saw this and said, "Do you want us to summon fire down out of heaven to consume them?" "Of course not!" I replied, "For the Son of Man has not come to destroy men's lives, but rather, to save them." Those twelve men went everywhere I went; and because they had been with Me, they saw everything I did. They too were touching and healing men just as they had seen Me do.

Soon, we all met together the night before I was to be killed. It was the Passover. As we ate the bread, I explained to them that the bread represented My body that was to be

broken for them. When we drank of the fruit of the vine, I
told them this stood for My blood that was to be shed for all
mankind. My Father knows all things, even before it happens. He revealed to Me exactly what was coming, and He
also reminded Me that this was the reason I was born. At
first My emotions resisted the whole idea. In fact, the stress
intensified so much that blood came out of the pores of My
skin. In that moment My Father's Spirit was there. His
Spirit helped Me and I was able to put My complete trust
in Him. After all, I reasoned, He had brought Me this far
and He would also give Me all I needed to complete the
purpose for which I came.

Those people who hated Me came to the garden late
that night to arrest Me. I just let them take Me because I
loved them anyway and I knew how much more My Father
loved them. They began to mock Me and to beat Me. They
yanked out huge portions of My beard. They brought Me
before the temple high priest to lay their charges against Me.
They made up lies about Me to condemn Me. But when
their lies became evident, the temple high priest inquired
of me directly, to plainly tell him if I was who I had made
myself out to be. He was so infuriated when I told him, "It
is as you say." He had me taken before two rulers, who
couldn't even decide what to charge me with. The temple
high priest demanded the rulers to have My life exchanged
for one of the prisoners who was sentenced to die. So I was
condemned. I took his place.

To humiliate Me, they took off My clothes, then they
beat My face and My body so much so that the skin on My
back, arms, and legs was torn open and blood poured out
everywhere. Then they platted a crown of thorns, pushing
it down firmly on My head, and spat on Me. They put on
a purple robe and yelled, "Hail, O great and mighty King."
My face was so battered, bruised, and bloodied that you
couldn't even tell it was Me.

Soldiers placed a huge cross upon My shoulder that was
so heavy I could hardly walk. I carried it through a narrow

and crowded street that led us out of the city. Finally, as I lost every ounce of strength and energy, as one of the guards pushed and I fell to the ground and gashed open one of My knees. In order to keep moving, they let another man carry the cross for Me until we got to the place of death. The hillside looked just like a big skull. The soldiers pounded nails through the base of My hands, fastening them to the crossbeam. They nailed My feet to the pole and hoisted the cross to an upright position until it went into the ground. It was awful and so painful that I could hardly breathe.

The worst of what occurred was when I could no longer sense My Father's presence anywhere. I called out to Him, "Daddy! Daddy, where are You?" But there was nothing, nothing at all, only silence.

There were two men one on either side of Me who also were to be crucified. One said, "If You really are who the people are shouting out that You are, and You have such power, then why don't You get us down from here?" The other said, "We are at the point of death and you still aren't afraid of God's judgment for your soul? We are guilty and we deserve our punishment, yet this man is innocent. Please, remember me, Yeshua, when You come into Your kingdom." Then I said, "Today you will be with Me in paradise."

By then I could hardly breathe at all because of the difficult position I was in. Finally, when I took My last breath, I said, "Abba, it is finished; into Your hands I commit My Spirit." A few hours later a soldier came by and thrust a spear deep into My side, piercing My heart to make sure I was dead. Blood and water began gushing out everywhere.

My mother, My brothers, and My friends came to take My body down from the cross to bury it. A man named Joseph had prepared a tomb and came to take My body for burial. Joseph wrapped My body in linen and quickly laid it in the tomb.

When death came to claim My body, I went down deep into the lower parts of the earth, where I remained there until the third day. While I was there, I proclaimed liberty to the captives who were bound in the prison of death. Since I had remained sinless and had fulfilled the will of My Father during My lifetime, death had no legal hold on Me.

By the third day My Father resurrected Me unto the fullness of all power in heaven, in earth, and under the earth. During that time I defeated the enemy of mankind, the evil one, the god of this world, Satan, and I took possession of the keys of death and hell. I then set the captives free and spoiled all principalities and powers of darkness. I triumphed over them and made an open and public spectacle of their utter defeat. Next, I paraded our stripped and defeated enemy Satan before the entire host of heaven. And in having gained the victory I, as a man and the Son of God, retain full authority in heaven, in earth, and under the earth, as well as over death and hell.

Although the angels rejoiced and shouted praises of victory all around Me, I knew that I must stop to bring encouragement to My friends before I went to see My Father. On the morning of the third day, when My mother and two other women came to the tomb and they saw that the stone to the tomb had been rolled away, they went to look in. When they looked in, there were two angels who proclaimed, "He is not here, but has risen." They ran back to where the men were to tell them what they had seen. Mary went back to the tomb with Peter and John, but Peter and John ran on ahead. John outran Peter and reached the tomb first. He looked inside and saw linen clothes lying there but did not go in. Then Peter came and went into the tomb and saw linen clothes lying in one place but the facial napkin was in another place. John then came in; and when he saw everything where it was laid, he believed. They still didn't understand that I was to rise from the dead.

As soon as they saw all of this, Peter and John left for their own homes thinking on all they had seen. Then Mary came to the tomb. Still thinking My body had been stolen, she stood outside the tomb weeping. When she stooped down to look inside, she saw two angels in white sitting *where My body had lain. They said, "He is not here!" She still didn't understand what the angels meant, for she said, "They have taken away my Lord and I don't know where they have put Him." Then I came and stood behind her. She heard Me and turned around, but she didn't know who I was. Then I said, "Why do you weep? Who are you looking for?" She thought I was the gardener and said, 'Sir, if you have taken Him, tell me where you have put Him." I said, "Mary!" She straightened up and turned around and recognized Me. She ran to Me and fell down and worshiped at My feet and started to grab Me, but I told her not to touch Me yet because I had not ascended to My Father. "Go to My brothers and tell them I ascend to My Father and your Father, and to My God and your God." Mary went and found the disciples and told them all that I had said.*

Then Yeshua finally said,

Oh, My beloved, when I went to see My Father, what a joyful time We had and as the scripture says,

What is man that You are mindful of him, and the son of [earthborn] man that You care for him? Yet You have made him but a little lower than God…, and You have crowned him with glory and honor. You made him to have dominion over the work of Your hands; You have put all things under his feet.

—PSALM 8:4–6, AMPC

Since the very beginning, I had been with My Father, and now it was so wonderful to be with Him again. The blood that had spilled forth from My body, My Father had it gathered and brought up to the mercy seat that is in His throne room. Applying that blood to the mercy seat was the entire purpose of My being born and why I died. My blood was the poured out sacrifice to pay for the penalty of your sins and the sins of the world, to remove the guilt, and to eliminate the shame for having committed those sins. The penalty for sin is death. The reason I had to die was so that

I would take your place in death. And because I took your place in death, when it comes time for you to face death, as all people must, you are now able to enter into My Father's presence and enjoy eternal life with Me, and My Father.

My Father was fully satisfied with all that I had done and said, "Go back and reveal to your friends who you are." When it was time, I went back and appeared to My friends so they could see Me again and to prepare them for My work there on earth as I would begin to flow through them. They almost didn't recognize Me. I spoke to them, and encouraged them to have faith believing who I am and who My Father is. They still didn't understand completely why I had come, except that their lives would never be the same. What had happened to Me would change their lives forever.

I spent many days talking to them and teaching them about kingdom living and instructing them how to teach others. I told them My Father's Spirit would soon come to take My place in the earth. He would bring to their remembrance all I had taught them, and also He would comfort and encourage those who remained steadfast in faith. But most important I told them that I would come again as the King of kings and Lord of lords to rule and reign and bring the kingdom of My Father to earth.

Then I ascended up in a cloud to My Father. Two of My Father's messengers standing by said, "The same way Yeshua, the Messiah, the Christ ascended into heaven He will come again."

Finally Yeshua said,

Now, My beloved, I, Yeshua Adonai, and My Father have made a covenant with each other on your behalf. My Father has given unto Me all of His authority. He has also given into My hands the fulfillment of all His Word. I came to fulfill His Word, and I did so when I was crucified for you, and in your behalf justifying you to the Father for all your sin and providing you with My righteousness that you may reign with Me on My throne forever.

When sin is committed, a curse of death falls upon that person who commits the sin because the sentence for that sin is death. When you receive Me, Yeshua, as your Savior and Lord, as you commit sin and ask My Father for forgiveness, instead of receiving the curse for that sin upon yourself, I have already received the curse for you. I took upon Myself all the curses when I was crucified. I paid the debt you owed that was caused by your having sinned. It was paid by My having accepted the penalty of sin for you. Now you can be free, instead of being under the sentence of death, which is eternal separation from the Father.

My blood that was placed on the mercy seat still keeps that covenant today, which the Father and I have made with each other for you. My blood causes the curse of eternal death to "pass over" you, and you are forgiven.

Then Yeshua said to me,

I call you My beloved; and, My beloved, I need you to be My best friend. Now that you have My Spirit within you, wherever you go and whatever you do when you call on My name, Yeshua, I will be there for you immediately. My Spirit will also teach you and remind you of all that I have spoken to you. My Spirit will also encourage you and lift you up.

This day was only the beginning of my new life with Yeshua. We meet every morning and every evening. We talk about everything under the sun. He is truly my best friend. He gave me a book about His life and about His Father and about all the other people who know Him personally, a book about our covenant with each other and with the Father. Now I go about my life telling others about my relationship with Yeshua, and about all the peace, joy, and love I always wanted and finally have. I feel so complete now.

Yeshua came to me one morning and said,

Let's go on a journey together. We are going to a special place, a secret place, where we can get to know each other better. You are My beloved and I love you, and I will never leave you nor will I forsake you. Even if you don't see Me,

rest assured, I will come at your calling. However, you must
watch out for those two thieves in particular, doubt and
unbelief, who come to steal your faith in Me and My abili-
ties and which can also destroy your peace.

So we began our journey of love and faith. In our journey we
came to a place where there was a thick forest of trees, so dense
that the sun was almost completely blocked out. There was a thick
undergrowth of vines so heavy that I could hardly go any further.
I pulled and pulled to remove the brush covering the path. It was
very difficult just to see the pathway that we were to go through. I
started to pull and pull on the undergrowth, but I could not break
up the tangled vines. I felt so angry and so frustrated.

Finally Yeshua came and asked, "*Would you like for Me to do that*
for you?" He instantly cut through all the thick underbrush and all
the thick vines that blocked our way. He said,

> *These represent the thick growth of anger and bitterness*
> *and frustration and resentment that is lodged in your heart;*
> *they must be removed. They are there because of sin in*
> *your heart and people in your past that hurt and wounded*
> *you. To remove the hurt you must forgive those people and*
> *release that anger, that bitterness, that frustration, and that*
> *resentment and give these feelings all to Me. I receive them*
> *from you now, and I replace those emotions with My love*
> *and My mercy and My forgiveness and My grace. Open*
> *your heart fully unto Me that I may come in to all parts to*
> *cleanse and purify your heart. Anger, bitterness, and unfor-*
> *giveness are some of the negative emotions that stand in*
> *the way to a pure and clean heart. You must surrender all*
> *those feelings to Me. Your heart is what I can truly talk to.*
> *I must have all your heart, for understand that I am jealous*
> *and I must have your whole heart.*

We continued on our journey to a new place that seemed to
descend to a lower elevation. In this place it appeared as though
we were entering a valley because I could see higher areas on both

sides. As we went further Yeshua said, "*I must now show you these high places.*"

When I looked up, there were huge stone statues all along the hillsides and in the valley. I said, "What are these?" He answered,

> *These are the idols that you are worshipping; they are people and things that you love more than you love Me. It grieves Me that you put them before Me.*

"O Yeshua, please forgive me," I replied. "I did not realize that I had been doing this." He replied,

> *You must now desire for them to come down out of your heart and put Me first. It is written in My Father's Word that King Asa took away the altars of the strange gods and the high places and broke down the images and cut down the groves and commanded Yudah to seek the Lord God of their fathers and to do the law and the commandments. Also he took away the high places and the images out of all the cities of Yudah and the kingdom was quiet under him.*

Then Yeshua went on to say,

> *An idol is anything that is more important to you in your life than God. If you can't live without a person or a thing in your life, then you have an idol. They are taking My place in your life. Who is God in your life? In the Book of 1 Kings, chapter 18, verses 37–39, Elijah the prophet cried out to My Father to reveal Himself to the people of Yishrael when he said,*

> "Hear me, O LORD, hear me, that this people may know that You are the LORD God, and that You have turned their hearts back to You again." Then the fire of the LORD fell and consumed the burnt sacrifice, and the wood and the stones and the dust, and it licked up the water that was in the trench. Now when all the people saw it, they fell

on their faces; and they said, "The Lord, He is God! The
Lord, He is God!"
                                    —1 Kings 18:37–39

*Therefore they no longer followed after the god Baal but
turned back to the great and mighty God.*

I exclaimed, "I command all these idols to come down in the
name and the blood of Yeshua Adonai." When I did this, I felt such
pain and such a great loss. But Yeshua was right there the entire
time with me to heal my pain and to comfort me in my loss. I then
realized He really is all I need.

He put His arms around me and held me. He whispered,

I love you; I love you!

He did so over and over again. When I had recovered enough, we
began to walk on further. We came to the edge of a clearing. When
I looked up ahead, all I could see was desert. I said, "Do I have to go
this way? Isn't there some other way?" He answered,

*No, there is no other way. If you want our relationship to
grow, you must walk through this place. However, I will
send helpers to walk with you. They are My closest of
friends. They are named Grace and Mercy.*
  *They will be there to hold you up until you get through to
the other side. For now I must go before you and meet you
at the next meeting place. No matter what, remember our
covenant. You will find out who I am in this place. Here
are food and water for you to start out with.*

So we started out on our journey to the other side. With me was
Grace on one side and on the other was Mercy. I tried not to look
too far off into the distance because it looked like this desolate place
was never ending. I kept my eyes on the immediate surroundings
and where we were at this present moment. As I looked around, it
seemed as though I had new eyes. Even though there was only sand
all around, everything in sight somehow became beautiful. I began
to see new colors in the hills on either side of me as well as in the

sparse tufts of grass and the thin spindly trees. We walked for what seemed like endless days until we came to an oasis. Trees were there all around and there was a pond that was fed by a natural spring. As we came near we saw that Yeshua was already there, waiting to meet us. He said,

> This quiet, restful place is to remind you that I am your source. When you are hungry or thirsty, I will be your supply.

He had already prepared for us some meat and fruit of all kinds. The water was so cool and pure tasting. It was all very refreshing. Again He reminded me that He will supply all my needs. Yeshua pointed to the source where the natural spring was coming up out of the rocks, and then He said,

> Within you there is a natural spring, a source of living water. Within you there is a deep well, and at the bottom of the well that source of living water flows. That living water is the Holy Spirit which flows deep within you. That water is My love which comes from the Father. But when you have anger, bitterness, unforgiveness, strife, and contention in your heart, it's like stones and boulders stuffed into your well. The flow of water, My Spirit, is stopped. You must come to Me in all honesty and repent of all these sins; then I can remove the stones and boulders, so, My love and My giftings can flow. My Holy Spirit can only fully be released by My love flowing through you. My Word says, "Faith works by love." Faith only has power through My love working through you.

Yeshua stopped and thought a moment and said,

> Just like Isaac had to re-dig his father Abraham's wells that had been stopped up through strife and contention, your spiritual wells can be stopped up. But when you repent I will unstop them so the Spirit can flow in all of His fullness. The Holy Spirit also wants to flow in signs and wonders and miracles through you. These are called the gifts

of the Holy Spirit and He can only truly flow in freedom
through vessels that are open and flowing freely. When you
come closer to Me and My love with an intimate relation-
ship with Me, I will bring you to the place of surrender. As
you grow less and less fearful of being open before Me, not
trying to cover your sins like Adam and Eve did, I will heal
your soul and remove the clutter from your wells. Thus your
wells will become fountains overflowing with My love and
those wells and fountains will have an endless supply of love
that others will come and drink from."

Yeshua hugged me and said, "*Now, I have to go. I will see you at*
another appointed time." Then He turned and walked away.

Grace and Mercy said, "It's time to go. Be aware, there are some
things that we will encounter along the way." We carried along with
us some of the fruit and water, because we were heading out in the
heat of the day. We walked until late in the afternoon. As I looked
out over the horizon, I saw a thick, dark cloud. Soon we were able
to determine that it was not just a cloud. Whatever it was, it seemed
to be moving toward us and was becoming frightfully ominous. Fear
seemed to grip me, and so I hung on tight to Grace and Mercy.

In a matter of minutes it was upon us. It came with a stench of
hot sulfuric air that almost took my breath away. There were five
of them and the fear they brought clawed at my insides. They were
of great muscular build and at least seven feet tall with pitch black
eyes that if you could look into them you would see hell. Their skin
was black and leathery with arms that hung down to the knees and
huge hands that could crush you in an instant. They spoke to me in
an eerie voice, saying, "We are all the things that you fear most. We
are going to steal your joy and your peace; and then we are going to
kill you!"

I became so frightened that all I could do was shake and tremble.
Then I said, "I was afraid this would happen." As I hung on tight to
Grace, I said, 'I don't know what to do."

Grace responded, "What did the Master say?"

"Well," I responded, "He said to call on His name." So I cried out,

Yeshua Adonai! Help me! My enemy is too great for me. Help!

In an instant Yeshua was there, and the forces of darkness had to leave. In His presence, they turned around and instantly fled off in every direction. Those creatures were afraid of Him. It was just awesome! Yeshua said,

> *Those were your fears that were hidden away in your heart. My perfect love has cast out all your fears because I took them on and have already defeated all the forces of darkness so that you could be free. I will continue to pour in more of My love each time you encounter fearful situations. As you trust in Me instead of the circumstances, you will continue to become freer because you will have more of Me. The Father's Word says to draw close to God and He will draw close to you; resist the devil and he will flee.*

Ever so grateful I said, "Oh thank You, Yeshua! Thank You so very much. I just want to praise Your name all the time." He put His arms around me and held me tight; and He said, "*I love you.*" As He held me, I was restored and refreshed. He said,

> *It's time you rested awhile. I will build a fire here to warm you, and I will cover you with My robe of righteousness. I have here for you some cool fresh water and food to refill you. They will give you new energy. As you eat this bread, let it remind you that I have already paid the price for your life with the sacrifice of My own body. Nothing can harm you or steal your life away from Me because I have already paid the price so that you might have life and have it more abundantly. No one can take that life from you, so you don't have anyone or anything to fear again.*

For the first time I slept without any fear whatsoever, comforted, knowing that I was totally protected resting in His loving arms. When I awoke, there was such love and peace and joy in my heart because of Him.

Grace and Mercy said to me, "Yeshua had to go on ahead to the next place of meeting. He always goes to prepare a place for you, and He is always where you need Him the most." When I closed my eyes, I could sense His presence still there, holding me in His arms.

Grace and Mercy said, "It's time to be moving on." I looked way out, far into the distance and saw something green. Perhaps we would soon be coming out of this desolate wasteland. I began getting excited. Seeing that green foliage, or whatever it was, was just so encouraging.

CHAPTER 2

TRUE LOVE

I SPOKE OF MY love for Yeshua to Grace and Mercy,

My beloved Savior is mine, and I am His.
He is everything I need.
He provides for me in every possible way.
He is my strength and my shield.
He hides me in a place of safety far from my enemy.
He fights my battle for me, well before I even approach
    the enemy.
He prepares the pathway for me, and He makes ready for
    me a table in the very presence of my enemies.
Oh, how wonderful and how beloved He is to me.
He is my ultimate delight.
Let Him kiss me with the sweetness of His lips, for His
    kisses are sweeter than wine.
And I will praise His glorious name, Yeshua, forever.

Grace and Mercy said that I had truly understood one of the most important kingdom keys. "Oh yes?" I asked, "What's that?"

They said, "Praise for Yeshua." They added, "Yeshua is preparing you for His wedding, as you are to be His bride, but for now, we must move on."

Joy burst in my heart as I thought upon all that they had said. Yeshua wants me to be His bride!

The way began to be a little rocky, and my footing was not too sure. As we moved on, it became obvious that we were getting close to some difficult places that ascended higher and higher. Grace and Mercy climbed first, and then pulled me up after them.

I began to complain about the rugged terrain and the heat of the

day. I began really feeling sorry for myself, and then complained
some more until I became angry with everything and everyone
around me. Grace and Mercy stopped and looked at me and said,
"If you keep this up, you'll restrain our hands and we won't be able
to help you. The enemy will then steal your faith and joy. Remember
your covenant with the Master."

I cried out,

> Oh no! Yeshua help me! I'm falling into sin.

Immediately, He was right there to help pull me out and up to
the next level. I looked at Him and said,

> Yeshua, please forgive me. I was so self-centered, only
> thinking of myself. Please, cleanse my heart again and
> remove from it that selfish and self-centered part.

Yeshua smiled and said,

> You're forgiven, My beloved. And yes, I will heal your heart
> and cleanse it. May I call you My beloved? For you are My
> beloved. I have prepared this resting place for you so that
> you can get refreshed again. Here is My bread, some of My
> fruit, and My cool refreshing water.

I responded,

> Oh, thank You so much for all of this! It's all so refreshing
> to me, but it is Your presence that is the most refreshing of
> all. Thank You for having come to my rescue.

We rested there for the remainder of the night. In the morning
I was totally refreshed. Grace and Mercy reminded me that it was
time to move on. We began climbing again, but this time my attitude
was one of joy and peace. This time I was the one on top, helping.

We finally came to a clearing where we saw a fire going. Yeshua was
sitting there, cooking fish. I ran over to Him and gave Him a huge
embrace. I was so glad to see Him! He waved His hand and said,

> Sit down and eat. Here's some cool fresh water and bread
> to eat with your fish.

After we finished eating, Yeshua and I walked over among the trees. Some of them were about twenty feet tall, and others were not even as tall as I am. Then Yeshua said,

> *These trees are illustrations of the trees that are in your heart. Some of the trees in your heart are those planted by the enemy before I saved you. These trees are pride, jealousy, envy, hatred, bitterness, and covetousness, just to name a few. But the Father wants to replace them with the fruit of His character of love, joy, peace, patience, kindness, goodness, long-suffering, meekness and faith. These are trees of His righteousness. He has been doing this from the time you began to resist the forces of darkness and submitted yourself to the Father's will. There is another place you must go through to continue the work that has been started. As you yield your emotions to Me and as you continue on with Grace and Mercy, they will lead you on down the path that I have chosen.*

We went down the road that He spoke of and there were many people passing us by. I could see sadness on their faces, as though they had no peace and needed a friend.

When I would try to tell them about my Yeshua, they would laugh at me or just ignore me as if I wasn't even there. I kept trying to tell them about Yeshua and His peace and how He made me free, but they responded by yelling and cursing at me. Their sharp words were so bitter, cutting, and hateful. I was merely trying to help, but they were all so cruel. I felt wounded and rejected. I tried to go on; but feeling so humiliated, bruised, and battered, I just broke down and wept.

Grace and Mercy reminded me of the covenant with the Master, so again, I called on His name, "Yeshua!"

He came instantly and comforted me. He reminded me of how He was rejected and despised by men.

> *These are your emotions and they must be given completely to Me. Your emotions are defensive, wanting to protect and shield you. You must surrender your emotions so that I may*

replace them with My emotions. My emotions come from the Father and they will be alive in you. Those emotions are loving, giving, self-sacrificing, and selflessness, where others' needs are more important than your own. Along with love are joy, peace, patience or long-suffering, kindness, goodness, faithfulness, gentleness, and self-control. Against such things there is no law that can bring a charge against you. These are My emotions and they will live in you when you surrender your own emotions to Me. Those people out there are lost and empty inside. They are little blind children who have lost their way. I came to give them life, and I need you to be My ambassador to touch them for Me. You must be willing to do just as I have done, and be willing to go so far as to give up your life for them, if necessary. They need to know about Me, and what I have done for them. I have already paid the price for them, and all they need to do is to believe and trust in Me. If they will believe and call on My name, as you have learned to do, they too can be free and have peace, just like you.

Yeshua, thank You so much for helping me understand. I think I can go back out there now and try again.

Yeshua then told me,

Now I will send you another Helper to walk alongside with you, and His name is Wisdom.

CHAPTER 3

THE DECEIVER

❧

W E WENT BACK on the way, and again there were people of all sorts with whom I met. I began to tell the people about my Master. Then I met a certain man, the most handsome I had ever met—next to my Master. He said all the right things that made me feel loved and accepted.

Wisdom spoke up and warned me. "Be careful with this one. Don't be too hasty about getting involved with him. Something is not right." I told Wisdom I didn't want to hear that and that I would make up my own mind and make my own decisions. I responded with what was on my mind, "Excuse me please, if you don't mind, I would rather do it my own way."

I told this handsome man all about my Yeshua; but he said, "What do you need Him for. I can do for you just as good as He can. Why don't you follow me instead, for I have all the money, power, prestige, position, social standing, and anything anyone could ever want."

I said, "That sounds absolutely great to me."

But all of my joy and peace seemed to go. I began to lose vitality, and my strength seemed to leave me. I felt as if I were dying. Wisdom finally brought to my attention my covenant with Yeshua, "Call on the Master, Yeshua, the Savior."

I cried out,

Oh Yeshua, help me, I'm dying! Please help me!

Yeshua was right there with me. I could hardly look Him straight in the eyes knowing how many times I've had to ask this very same thing before:

Oh forgive me, Yeshua; this time for wanting to do things my own way. Forgive me for wanting to exalt my own will above Yours.

Yeshua responded immediately,

You are forgiven and your sin is washed away by My blood.

I said,

Yeshua, now help me to forgive myself for committing this most horrible of sins.

Yeshua told me,

It's already being done,

I then asked,

Yeshua, my Beloved, I love You so much; but how can You keep forgiving me for all the awful things I've done?

He answered,

Never be afraid or ashamed to ask for forgiveness for your sins. My Father and I hate sin, but We love you. All men have sinned and come short of the Father's requirements for righteousness, but that was why I came. I took all those sins upon Myself and was crucified so that you might be at peace, free from guilt and shame.

Oh Yeshua, You are truly my Beloved Savior, and how I do love You. You are my shield and my protection. How can I be afraid, or how can I be ashamed? You are everything I need, and You are my provider. I love You so very much.

Yeshua said,

He that tried to draw you away from Me was the seducer, also known as the deceiver. He was sent by the enemy of your soul, Satan, the god of this world, to draw you away from Me. He was sent to take your focus off Me and to put

*your love on the things of the world. The love of this world
brings death to your spirit, but your love and faith in Me
bring eternal life.*

*You have learned an important lesson here. My Father's
Word speaks of how Lucifer, now called Satan, was a heavenly angel of God who was the cherub who covered the mercy
seat. My Father said in the Book of Ezekiel, chapter 28:*

Thus says the Lord God: You are the full measure and pattern of exactness [giving the finishing touch to all that con-
stitutes completeness], full of wisdom and perfect in beauty.
You were in Eden, the garden of God; every precious stone
was your covering, the carnelian, topaz, jasper, chrysolite,
beryl, onyx, sapphire, carbuncle, and emerald; and your
settings and your sockets and engravings were wrought
in gold. On the day that you were created they were prepared. You were the anointed cherub that covers with over-
shadowing [wings], and I set you so. You were upon the
holy mountain of God; you walked up and down in the
midst of the stones of fire [like the paved work of gleaming
sapphire stone upon which the God of Israel walked on
Mount Sinai]. You were blameless in your ways from the
day you were created and iniquity and guilt were found in
you. Through the abundance of your commerce you were
filled with lawlessness and violence, and you sinned; therefore I cast you out as a profane thing from the mountain
of God and the guardian cherub drove you out from the
midst of the stones of fire. Your heart was proud and lifted
up because of your beauty; you corrupted your wisdom for
the sake of your splendor. I cast you to the ground; I lay
you before kings that they might gaze at you. You have
profaned your sanctuaries and the enormity of your guilt,
by the unrighteousness of your trade. Therefore I have
brought forth a fire from your midst; it has consumed you,
and I have reduced you to ashes upon the earth in the sight
of all who looked at you.

—EZEKIEL 28:12–18, AMPC

The Word also says in Isaiah,

> How you have fallen from heaven, O light-bringer and
> daystar, son of the morning! How you have been cut
> down to the ground, you who weakened and laid low
> the nations.... And you said in your heart, I will ascend
> to heaven; I will exalt my throne above the stars of God;
> I will sit upon the mount of assembly in the uttermost
> north. I will ascend above the heights of the clouds; I will
> make myself like the Most High. Yet you shall be brought
> down to Sheol (Hades), to the innermost recesses of the
> pit.... Those who see you will gaze at you and consider you,
> saying, Is this the man who made the earth tremble, who
> shook kingdoms?—Who made the world like a wilderness
> and overthrew it's cities, who would not permit his pris-
> oners to return home?
>
> —ISAIAH 14:12–17, AMPC

I was just the opposite. I became obedient by the things I
suffered so that I was able to say, "Not my will but thy will
be done." Because of this completed experience, I became
the author and source of eternal salvation to all those who
give heed and obey Me. I then became my Father's High
Priest for His people, after the order of Melchizedek. Now
I stand before the Father forever making prayer, petitions,
and intercession for you.

Then Yeshua said,

Please come and rest in My presence. Let us go now to the
secret place, My garden.

CHAPTER 4

THE GARDEN (WISDOM ABOUT THE BATTLE)

༄

BEFORE I COULD turn around, we were in a beautiful garden. There was a field just ahead of beautiful flowers of lavender and purple. We walked through the field of flowers, and it was more than my eyes could take in. The garden was so glorious and stretched as far as the eye could see. Yeshua said,

> *I just want to refresh you and encourage you so that you can go on and not faint or lose heart. My beloved, you are so special to Me.*

He stood facing me, and put His hands on both sides of my face. He looked deep into my eyes and spoke softly,

> *You are a joy and a delight to Me just as you are. I love the way your eyes light up when you smile. You don't have to be any certain way to please Me. You please Me just as you are.*

I responded,

> *Thank You for encouraging me. Sometimes I have thought that I wasn't good enough, or didn't do the right things, or that I made so many mistakes.*

Yeshua said,

> *You won't ever have to measure up, because I am He who is worthy. I was able to measure up for you, for it was I who accomplished all that was necessary to pay the price for you. It was because of the righteousness of my Father that when*

I was on the cross I poured out my blood so my Father accepted my sacrifice for you. When you accept Me as your Savior and Lord, the Father imparts to you His righteousness. In actuality, I have made you acceptable. Now you can accept yourself as one who is worthy because I have made you worthy. I don't condemn you for your mistakes, because it's all by my Father's grace—your faith in Me and what I've done for you. It's only Satan, the enemy of your soul, who condemns and accuses you; and as long as you give him no place, he remains powerless beneath your feet.

We began to walk until we came to an ocean with a sandy beach. Yeshua and I walked in the sand along the seashore and let the waves wash over our feet. It was so good to be here with Him. I said, "You know, I just love the ocean and anywhere there's water."

Yeshua responded, *"Yes, I know. That's why I brought you here."*

I looked out across the water and saw the sun as it was beginning to set. I said,

I don't want to leave this place, because it's so glorious and so good being here with You. I want to thank You so much for thinking of me.

He said, *"You know, we must go on to the next place."*

I responded, "I know." Yeshua then said,

Before we go, it's time that I teach you about spiritual warfare and about going forth in the world as My ambassador and about your being My instrument of blessing, so that through you I may reach the unsaved and heal those who are hurting. Let Me show you your armor and how to put it on.

He explained,

First, you put on the belt of truth, for My Father's truth endures forever. It is written in the Word that I, Yeshua the Christ, am the way, the truth, and the life. No one comes to the Father, but by Me. With the Father's word of truth

you can stand against the wiles of the devil. You can't stand upon your own truth which is of the world, because that truth is sinking sand and has no foundation. Only I am the rock that you can stand on. Only the Father's loving-kindness and truth in His Word will continually preserve you. The Father desires truth in your inward parts and in the hidden part the Father will make you to know wisdom.

When you know the truth of who you are and My Father's Word, then Satan can't overwhelm you. Therefore, gird up the loins of your mind with truth, be sober, and rest your hope fully upon the grace of God that is brought to you at the revelation of the Christ.

The greatest truth that will keep you is that the Father will never leave you nor forsake you and that the Father is always faithful. If anyone sins and confesses and turns from this sin, I speak to the Father in your defense because of the righteousness of My Father which dwells in Me and you. I was the atoning sacrifice for your sins, but also for the sins of the whole world. When you learn of Me and My ways, you will know the truth. For truth is in Me.

You are to put off the old self, which was being corrupted by its deceitful false desires. Be made new in the attitudes of your minds and put on the new self, created to be like God the Father in true righteousness and holiness. When you speak the truth in love, you will in all things grow up into Me, the Head. From Me, the Christ, the whole body is joined and held together by every supporting ligament, which grows and builds itself up in love as each part does its work. The Father is Spirit, and you must worship Him in Spirit and in Truth. Therefore you rid yourselves of all such things as these; anger, rage, malice, slander, and filthy language from your lips. Do not lie to one another, since you have taken off your old self with its practices, and have put on the new self, which is being renewed in knowledge in the image of its Creator. For God's truth will be like a shield and buckler to protect you from the evil one. The belt of truth carries the weapons for battle.

Yeshua continued,

> Next you put on the breastplate of My righteousness, so
> that your heart will be protected. Therefore, you can have
> a pure heart to make godly decisions. This righteousness is
> the Father's righteousness. The Word says God's righteous-
> ness is an everlasting righteousness and His law is truth.
>
> The Word of God also says, the righteousness of God
> delivers from death. In the way of righteousness is life, and
> in its pathway there is no death. In the Lord Jehovah you
> have righteousness and strength. The Word of God also
> says your own righteousness is of the law and it is cursed.
> The righteousness which is in Me is the righteousness that
> comes from God and is received by faith in Me, the Christ,
> the Messiah, the anointed One.
>
> In former days they fashioned a breastplate for making
> decisions. When the people needed a word from God, they
> put on the ephod which was like a breastplate. It wasn't for
> war but it was to receive wisdom from God. The breast-
> plate was set with twelve stones, each stone representing
> the twelve tribes. When they needed instruction from the
> Lord, they would ask a question and then would wait for an
> answer. The answer would come when one or more of the
> stones would receive a reflected light from the sun. But now
> you have received the righteousness of God which gives you
> a pure heart to receive directly from God.
>
> Solomon, the king who lived in former days, understood
> the righteousness of God. Because of this he asked of God
> for a discerning heart to govern God's people and to dis-
> tinguish between right and wrong. He needed grace and
> wisdom to govern God's great number of people."

Then Yeshua spoke again and said,

> In the Book of Jeremiah the Word says that Jehovah My
> Father shall be called Jehovah Tsidkenu, which is The Lord
> Our Righteousness. The Word also says that I, Yeshua, the
> Christ, the Messiah, the anointed One, am the end of the

law of righteousness to everyone who believes in Me. Therefore, you are the righteousness of God through Me.

But, if I, Yeshua, the Christ, the Messiah, am in you, your body is dead because of sin, yet your spirit is alive because of righteousness. It is because of the Father that you are in Me, Yeshua, the Christ, the Messiah, and I have become for you wisdom from the Father—that is your righteousness, holiness, and redemption. Again, it is spoken in the Word that in judgment we again be founded on righteousness, and all the upright in heart will follow God's righteousness. It is also written, our own righteousness is as filthy rags compared to God's righteousness.

Remember you can fight any battle and be victorious against temptation, sin, and the many attacks of our enemy Satan and his minions. But the victory is not because of any of your own goodness, but it's because of the righteousness and holiness of the Father who lives in Me. Now that I live in you, you receive the protection of the Father's righteousness against all enemies.

Yeshua continued,

Next, you put on your feet the shoes of the preparation and the knowledge of the gospel of peace. Your preparation for this last battle is the gospel about My life, death, and resurrection. My work here on earth brought you peace with My Father. This reconciliation through Me allows you to fight with boldness, confidence, perseverance, and peace.

Then Yeshua looked down at His own feet, saying,

My own feet were pierced; but as Yeshua, the Christ, the Messiah, I will never be moved. I am your firm foundation. Remember, since you have been justified through faith, you have peace with the Father through Me, the Christ, the Messiah, through whom you have gained access by faith into this grace in which you now stand. Therefore, I will make level paths for your feet and take you only on ways that are firm.

Again Yeshua said,

> *I am your strength and your song, for I am your salvation.*
> *As it is written,*

> My people will know my name; therefore in that day they
> will know that it is I who foretold it. Yes, it is I. How beau-
> tiful on the mountains are the feet of those who bring good
> news, who proclaim peace, who bring good tidings, who
> proclaim salvation, who say to Zion, "Your God reigns!"
> —ISAIAH 52:6–7, NIV

Following this, Yeshua said,

> *The shield of faith is the next piece of armor to put on. In*
> *the former days the shield was made out of laminated wood*
> *covered by leather and it was almost the size of the man*
> *who carried it. Shields were primarily for individual pro-*
> *tection and put together formed a wall of protection for the*
> *company. Soldiers with overlapping shields, which is called*
> *a Phalanx meaning unity, could continue advancing toward*
> *the gates of a city despite the arrows of the enemy. But the*
> *shield of faith of the Father is greater and more powerful*
> *than any earthly shield. By faith you are connected to My*
> *power and the shield of the Father will protect you from the*
> *slings and arrows of the enemy."*

Yeshua then said,

> *Satan's attacks come as insults, and temptations causing*
> *you to back up or be stymied in your progression, but the*
> *Father's shield of faith protects you from Satan's flaming*
> *arrows. Thus you will begin to see everything through God's*
> *eyes and His perspective and see beyond your circumstances*
> *and know the ultimate victory to be yours. The Father has*
> *armed you with strength for battle and has made your*
> *adversaries bow at your feet. He has made your enemies*
> *turn their backs in flight and has destroyed your foes. I have*
> *caused the enemy to lose heart; they come trembling from*

*their strongholds. I am the God who avenges you, who sub-
dues nations under you, who saves you from your enemies.
I have exalted you above your foes, from violent men I shall
rescue you. The only protection against the flaming arrows
that rain down from the sky in warfare is the shield of faith.
Your trust in Me alone as your shield is what will protect
you. You cannot rely on your own abilities in this battle.*

Yeshua then said,

*Now faith is being sure of what we hope for and certain of
what we do not see. By faith we understand that the universe was formed at God's command so that what is seen
was not made out of what was visible. Without faith it is
impossible to please God, because anyone who comes to
Him must believe that He exists and that He rewards those
who earnestly seek Him.*

Then Yeshua added,

*Those who came before you through faith, such as David the
King and Daniel, conquered kingdoms, administered justice, and gained what was promised; who shut the mouths
of lions, quenched the fury of flames, escaped the edge of the
sword; whose weakness was turned to strength; who became
powerful in battle and routed foreign armies."*

Yeshua followed up with this:

*Next, you put on the helmet of salvation. When going to
war the soldier put the helmet on his head to protect the
sides of the face, and there was a piece that protruded down
to cover the nose and pieces that covered the areas under
each eye. There was a shelf on the back of the helmet that
protected the neck and shoulders from arrows that fell from
above. The Word says,*

But since we belong to the day, let us be self-controlled putting on the faith and love as a breastplate, and the hope
of salvation as a helmet. For God did not appoint us to

suffer wrath but to receive salvation through our Lord
Jesus Christ.

—1 THESSALONIANS 5:8–9, NIV

*For by this gospel you are saved, if you hold firmly to the
Word that I preached to you. It is written,*

*O sovereign Lord, my strong deliverer, who shields my
head in the day of battle.*

—PSALM 140:7, NIV

*The Word also says you have the mind of Christ, for the
helmet of salvation covers and protects your mind from the
enemy's attacks. He can't have your mind if you stand on
the Word of God. Let this mind be in you which was also
in Yeshua the Christ. Therefore, since Christ suffered for us
in the flesh, arm yourselves also with the same mind, for he
who has suffered in the flesh has ceased from sin.*

Yeshua smiled and said,

*For though you live in the world, you do not wage war as the
world does. The weapons you fight with are not the weapons
of the world. On the contrary they have divine power to
demolish strongholds in the mind. You must demolish arguments and every pretension that sets itself up against the
knowledge of God, and you must take captive every thought
to make it obedient to Me, the Christ. Then you will no
longer be infants, tossed back and forth by the waves and
blown here and there by every wind of teaching and by the
cunning craftiness of men in their deceitful scheming.*

Yeshua went on to say,

*When I was crucified they put a crown of thorns upon My
head, which represented Satan's attempt to pierce the mind,
to destroy it. But I overcame every area and took dominion
over every sphere including the mind. When I went to the
cross and I arose from the dead, I stripped the devil, Satan,
and all his minions of their power, authority, and dominion*

over every domain. This includes the mind, will, and emotions; for I am King of kings, and Lord of lords over all. It is written,

For those who live according to the flesh set their minds on the things of the flesh, but those who live according to the Spirit, the things of the Spirit. For to be carnally minded is death, but to be spiritually minded is life and peace. Because the carnal mind is enmity against God; for it is not subject to the law of God, nor indeed can be. So then, those who are in the flesh cannot please God. But you are not in the flesh but in the Spirit, if indeed the Spirit of God dwells in you. Now if anyone does not have the Spirit of Christ, he is not His.

—ROMANS 8:5–9

Finally Yeshua said,

Take up the Sword of the Spirit which is the Word of God. In former days the soldier had two swords, one a small dagger that was put in a sheath attached to his belt, and the second type was a large two edged sword which was used for thrusting. I Yeshua, the Christ, am the Word of God. I was with the Father from the beginning. I, the Word became flesh, a human being, and dwelt among you. The Father, through the work on the cross, has made you a sharp sword as you speak the Word of God with your mouth. It is written, 'He made my mouth like a sharpened sword. In the shadow of His hand He hid Me; He made Me into a polished arrow and concealed Me in His quiver. For the Lord takes delight in His people; He crowns the humble with salvation. Let the saints rejoice in this honor and sing for joy on their beds. May the praise of God be in their mouths and a double-edged sword in their hands to wreak vengeance upon the nations and chastisement upon the peoples (demonic minions), to bind their kings (demons) with chains, and their nobles with fetters of iron, to execute upon them the judgment written. He the Lord is the honor of all

*His saints, Praise the Lord! For the Word of God is living
and active, sharper than any double-edged sword. It pen-
etrates even to dividing soul and spirit, joints and marrow,
it judges the thoughts and attitudes of the heart."*

Yeshua softened the tone of His voice and said,

*Remember to first submit yourself to God. Resist the devil
and he will flee from you. Come near to God and He will
come near to you. Before you go into battle be reminded that
the battle belongs to the Lord. It's not by your might, nor
by your power, but by the Holy Spirit. For the Lord your
God is the one who goes with you to fight for you against
your enemies to give you the victory. It is God who arms
you with strength and makes your way perfect. He makes
your feet like the feet of a deer. He enables you to stand in
high places. He trains your hands for battle so that your
arms can bend a bow of bronze. He gives you your shield of
victory and His right hand sustains you. The Father stoops
down to make you great. He broadens the path under you
so that your foot does not slip.*

*When you have equipped yourself, you are then ready
for battle against the forces of darkness. Always remember,
I am your armor, and it is I who protects you."*

Yeshua said,

*I need you to touch others for Me in your daily life. Others
need to know about Me because there are those out there
who are bruised, battered, wounded, imprisoned, and
hurting. Prepare your shields, both large and small, and
march out for battle! Harness the horses, mount the steeds!
Take your positions with helmets on! Polish your spears, put
on your armor! You must go into battle to snatch the souls
of men from the powers of darkness! Then they can begin
a relationship with Me, just as you have. The Father will
send His Spirit on ahead of you to prepare their hearts to
receive My Word that you speak.*

Then I said, "Tell me more about spiritual warfare." Yeshua responded,

> *In your journeys you will encounter strongmen who will attempt to intimidate you. But don't be afraid, because they must bow their knees when you speak My name, Yeshua, and when you speak My Word. They know who I am, and at My command, they have to go. When you command them in My name, they see Me standing there, and so they have to obey. They are terrified of My authority, because it is My Father who gave all authority into My hands. And I give you that authority and power to use My name. I also give you power and authority to tread on serpents and scorpions and over all the power of the enemy and nothing shall by any means hurt you. Are you ready to go into the battle with Me?*

I answered, "Yes, let's go!" Right then He reached forward to brush a strand of hair out of my face. For the first time I saw the horrible nail-pierced scar that extended from the base of His hand through the middle of His wrist. My eyes of understanding were suddenly open, and I was then able to somewhat realize the extent and price He had truly paid for saving my life and the lives of everyone else. It became very apparent His acquaintance with grief as He bore in His body the scars of having been bruised, battered, wounded, and hurt.

I said to Him,

> *What a friend I have in You, Yeshua. What a beloved and wonderful Savior You really are. For You are able to truly identify with the hurt and grief of all people. Thank You for loving us so much. Thank You for Your Mercy and Grace, and also Your Forgiveness and Loving Kindness.*

Then He did the most amazing thing. He reached down with those nail-scarred hands and ever so gently touched the scars and wounds on my legs that had been inflicted by the world.

When He did this it felt like warm soothing oil was being poured out all over me. All I could do was weep as every one of those past

wounds and scars were being removed and healed. He spoke to me
and said,

> You must forgive those who hurt you; I did. I was bruised
> for your iniquities: the chastisement of your peace was upon
> Me and with My stripes you were healed. I am the Good
> Shepherd who lays down His life for His sheep.

CHAPTER 5

UP THE MOUNTAIN

❧

YESHUA SAID TO me,

It's time for you to continue your journey again. We must go up the mountain. Remember, I'm always with you, even if I don't appear to be. My Spirit is always there and I have prepared the way for you. Wisdom and Faith will tell you all you need to know.

We began walking toward the mountain. I told everyone I met on the road about my Yeshua. We went further on down the road; suddenly there was an explosion right beside me. Faith and Wisdom then grabbed my hands and said, "We will walk you through, for this is the first part of the battle. Our enemy is aiming his weapons at you to bring fear back into your heart."

It seemed as if everywhere my foot stepped there was another explosion going off. It was as though we had walked into a minefield. But I knew Yeshua's Spirit was with me to protect me. I remembered His words saying,

Don't let fear take hold of you, for I am with you.

We made it through and past that area. Wisdom said to me, "It was your faith and trust in Yeshua that brought you through this area of your journey."

There was a woman on the road who was wounded, so I picked her up. When I poured into her wounds the oil of love and the wine of my Master, those wounds were healed. Further down the road there was a lame man. And again, healing ointment was poured out from my Master, Yeshua. When His love flowed out of me to these hurting and wounded people; it was like rivers of living water. It was just as though He was standing there instead.

We finally came to the base of the mountain and began to climb up. Wisdom helped me climb up over the large boulders that were in the way. The way was a little rough with the large rocks, and brush was everywhere, but we kept going. Then it began to get dark.

Wisdom said, "I believe we had better go this way." Just as we moved to one side, there appeared two evil-looking men. One of them said, "I am a thief, and I have come to take all that you have." In my mind, fear began trying to overwhelm me, but Yeshua's words came to mind:

Don't be afraid; I have prepared the way for you.

Faith said, "Use the name!" And I said, "In the name of Yeshua, you will not steal, kill, or destroy; and I command you to go now!" Immediately these two emissaries of darkness fell all over each other trying to get out of the way. Then instantly they were gone. It was so amazing.

Then Wisdom said, "Look, there is a cave where we can rest in over there." As we moved in that direction, I could see a flicker of light emanating from within the cave. My heart leaped within me, and I knew it was my beloved Yeshua. He was glad to see us. He had food already prepared for us after our difficult journey.

Everything tasted so good. And the water was so cool and refreshing. Yeshua came over to me and said, *"Let's take a walk outside."* When we stepped outside I was so overwhelmed at the brightness of the stars; because we were higher up, the stars were brighter, clearer, and more glorious. I looked deeply into Yeshua's face, and then He said,

I just wanted to tell you how much I love you. You are so important to Me. Thank you for giving all of yourself to Me. When you give yourself to Me, it generates such a sweet smelling fragrance. You are such a delight to Me, and I just wanted to tell you so. Everything about you is satisfying to Me.

His words touched me so deeply that I wept. I took in all of His words, for His word is like a refreshing breeze or a cool drink of water to a thirsty soul whenever He speaks. I responded by saying,

My beloved Savior I live off of every word You speak. You are the very life I live and whose air I breathe, Your word thrills my very being, and Your words are food for my spirit and soul and body.

Then I said,

Let Him kiss me with the kisses of His mouth! For Your love is better than wine. Because of the fragrance of You good ointments, Your name is as ointment poured forth, therefore do I love You.

Yeshua responded by saying,

You are the only one of your mother, Grace, for you were born from My Father's grace. When I say "only one" I speak of those who not only have been born of grace and the Spirit, but also those who hunger and thirst for intimacy and My love and have passion for Me. They have a passion, the flame of Yah, the flame of the love of the Lord; and they will not let anything separate them from that love for Me. For the Holy Spirit searches the hearts of those who have been touched by the Father and is looking for lovers and seekers who love Me for who I am and not for what they can get. The Holy Spirit is looking for a bride for Me who is in love with Me.

Then He put his arms around me and held me close. It was wonderful just to rest my head on His chest. We stood there like that for awhile, and then He lifted my head with His finger under my chin and gazed deeply into my eyes. When I looked into His eyes, I saw a glimpse of heaven, all shining and sparkling. But just for a moment did He let me see a little of eternity, for I almost fainted. Yeshua caught me and said,

It's almost time for Me to take My rightful place as King of the earth. Things are beginning to stir in My Father's house, and I just wanted you to know. It won't be long and we will be together throughout eternity.

I rested that night in the cave and woke up to a cloudy day.

CHAPTER 6

IN THE MIDST OF THE STORM

✣

ISDOM AND FAITH said, "We must continue on up the mountain." As the day wore on, the sky grew darker and more ominous. The wind started to blow harder and harder until we could hardly stand against it. Leaves, twigs, and branches were blowing everywhere around us. I became frightened at the strong wind and the stirring up that it was doing. Then it began to rain until we could barely walk.

Wisdom said, "Look, there is a hiding place in the rock. We went into the cleft of the rock, and Yeshua was there. When I saw Him I ran to Him and He hugged me. I sang a song to Him from the Word, saying,

> The voice of my Beloved!
> Behold, he comes
> Leaping upon the mountain,
> Skipping upon the hills.
> My Beloved is like a gazelle or a young stag.
> Behold, he stands behind our wall.
> He is looking through the windows,
> Gazing through the lattice.
> —SONG OF SOLOMON 2:8–9

After smiling at Him with eyes full of love, I asked Him, "What is the meaning of this storm?" And He answered,

> *This is to show you that even in the midst of the greatest storm, I have a hiding place just for you, to protect you and defend you, and that even the greatest of calamities can't*

hurt you or touch you. I am your greatest defense; I am your protector.

Then Yeshua began to sing His Word back to me,

Rise up my love, my fair one, And come away. For, lo, the winter is past, The rain is over and gone. The flowers appear on the earth; The time of singing is come, And the voice of the turtledove is heard in our land. The fig tree puts forth her green figs, And the vines with tender grapes give a good smell. Rise up, my love, My fair one, And come away! O my dove, in the clefts of the rock, in the secret places of the cliff, Let Me see your face, Let Me hear your voice; For your voice is sweet, And your face is lovely.

—Song of Solomon 2:11–14

Then Yeshua spoke and said,

The winter I am talking about is a season of trials and tests. Now you have come through that season of winter of which the true life is hidden from yourself and others. That true life of hidden weaknesses and sins must be dealt with before the spring comes so that all your new fruit is good fruit. It's in the winter season that the husbandman comes to prune off all the unproductive branches, so that new fruit can come forth in the spring.

My heart cried out to Him,

O Yeshua, what would I ever do without You? You know everything I need even before I know it.

Yeshua responded,

Remember this always, I knew you even when you were in your mother's womb.

With humble adoration I said,

O how great You are, my Yeshua, my Beloved!

Then He said,

> *This experience has taken you up higher to the next level. In this next level, your faith and trust in Me will increase, as well as your love for Me. You are dying to your old self so that My love will flow more freely through you. I want to touch even the hardest of hearts through you.*

I was deeply touched by His words.

> *Yeshua, I want You to know that I love You so much, and I thank You for trusting in me, and seeing me through every situation.*

I then added,

> *Thank You for not ever letting me go; You are my life, my hope, my strength. Thank You for encouraging me and lifting me up when I am low.*

Yeshua told me,

> *It's time to move on up higher.*

So Wisdom, Faith, and I began our climb once again. The storm seemed to have cleared the air, because every breath I took was sweeter than the last. All the earth seemed more alive than before. I looked around and saw all the tree branches swaying in the breeze, and the songs of the birds were even clearer in my ears than ever before.

My whole outlook seemed to be freer than ever. I felt like a bird that had just been set free from a cage to soar. I felt like an eagle who was rising up and up, far above the clouds, with nothing to hold me down. Only the wind was able to direct my path. The air currents had pushed me so I was able to soar higher and higher. There was nothing to hold me down to the earth anymore.

Wisdom spoke up asking, "Will you be ready at the Master's calling to come and meet with Him?"

"Of course," I answered, "But just what exactly do you mean?"

CHAPTER 7

TOUCHING THE SECRET PLACE

✥

WISDOM RESPONDED, SAYING, "You now have come up high enough in your walk with Him that you may enter into His presence where He is. When He would like to speak with you, He will call you and then you may enter into His secret place. This place is special unto the Lord, His Majesty. This is where He shares His most secret thoughts and dreams—the place of revelation. It is the place where He will reveal His covenant truths to you."

"We must, however, move on further," Wisdom continued. We kept going higher and higher until we passed all the rocks and boulders. It appeared as though we entered into another place, unlike any other I had ever seen before. Flowers of every color, shade, and type, all so lovely, were all around; yellows, reds, and purples. Yeshua came walking up to us and said,

> Welcome to My secret place. This is the high place that I've been telling you about. You can see for miles at this point. There are many others like you who have made it to this place of My rest and peace. Whenever a storm or calamity is around you, you may come enter this place, take shelter, enter into My rest, and enjoy My perfect peace. Then you will be able to fulfill My purpose for your life.

Right there, for the very first time, I could see what my Yeshua really looked like. His skin tone was a light olive tan, and it had an almost rugged and coarse texture. He stood to be about six feet in height, with muscular and very sturdy arms, as though He could lift almost anything without effort. He was clad in a long white robe that had a wide gold belt about the waist. His midnight black hair reached to about His shoulders. Most importantly was His face, with chiseled features, a strong nose, and eyes that were large and so intense, as if He could see right through you or as if all things were transparent before Him. Beyond His intense gaze, there was a distinct and overwhelming sense of compassion in His eyes. And love just somehow radiated out of His entire being. That love emanating forth from Him was more like passion than a mere devotional type of love. The expression of His entire being could be summed up in two words: *divine passion.*

It was so good to be in His presence again, very fulfilling and satisfying. As He spoke to me, it was like the thunderous sound of many rushing waters. He said, *"I'm so glad you are here. I've been expecting you, and I would like to show you around."* Then He took my hand and said, *"Let's walk."* He guided me over to a large river. The source of the river was a giant waterfall flowing from a mountaintop. He told me,

This is the river of life.

And then He asked,

Isn't it beautiful?

He went on to say,

It flows down from My Father's throne. It brings life and healing to the nations. Everything draws life from this river of life. My Father has imparted unto Me the life-giving power that comes from this river of life. I have that water of life, and I have given it to you freely all this while. I want you to know how much I love you and care for you. My Father has planted such lovely fruit bearing trees in the soil of your heart. They are all pleasant to My taste. Thank you for having offered to Me all the fruit of those trees in your heart. I have gathered together all that fruit and accept it as your freewill love gift unto Me. The fragrance of all that fruit together is sweeter than the finest perfume. I am preparing you to be My bride.

My heart was about to burst in anticipation of what I felt He was about to say. The most wonderful words I have ever heard came right out of His mouth,

Will you be My bride?

By then my heart felt like it was about to explode with excitement. Then in a soft and loving voice, I answered Him with this song of love:

O Yeshua, my beloved Savior, how I love Thee.
My love for Thee comes springing up from deep within me,
Like a fountain bubbling up, joyful and splashing with
    merriment.
Thy love for me is complete; Thy love comforts me with its
    presence.
My face expresses unsurpassed joy at Thy pleasing
    countenance.

My Savior, Thou art everything to me.
My joy is full because I know without a doubt I am loved.
Everything I am belongs to Thee.
Thou speak Thy love words to me in soft and gentle
    whispers,
So thou can draw nearer to me.

Oh, what a joy Thou art unto me!
Praises spring forth out of my mouth,
And love rises effortlessly out of my heart for Thee.
I love to worship Thee as I bask in Thy presence.

But when Thou are not near to me,
Or Thy name is not on my lips,
My soul pants and longs after Thee
And my spirit yearns to be near to Thee.
To smell the sweetness of Thy breath again,
And the want of the glorious scent of Thy presence;
Be near me again.

If I wander away from Thee or am lost,
Thou throw Thy staff down and
Gird up Thy loins to come after me.
But how can I ever be lost
When thou art always alert, ever watchful?
How can I ever be lost
When my Beloved is my Savior, my Shepherd
My God, and my King?

I submit my love to Thee in completeness and joy.
My beloved Savior is my love never ending,
Fulfilled to overflowing and complete.

Of course! Yes!

I said. "Now I know I will never be the same. I'm promised to
Him. Oh, how glorious!" Then Yeshua said,

> *You've made the journey, and now you know how to over-
> come. It was My faith imparted unto you that enabled you
> to gain the victory. You overcome because of My blood and
> by My Word that you speak mixed with that faith. You
> must continue to keep your eyes on Me alone, and not on
> the circumstances around you. You are doing well and are
> victorious in me. You are walking by faith!*
>
> *Now that you have been to the mountain, you must go
> back and tell others and help others come to the moun-
> taintop. I know that you know how to win in every battle. I
> will call you from the mountain again and again in these last
> days. I want you to continue telling others that I am coming
> soon. You are only a breath away from My setting up My
> reign on this earth. You must be continually watching and
> waiting to hear My call, especially listening for the sound of
> the trumpet. Everyone in My Father's kingdom is preparing
> for this day. They are preparing everything for the wedding
> supper. Also they are preparing for the final battle against
> the powers of darkness.*

Then He said to me,

> It's time for you to go. I love you, and I will wait earnestly
> expecting our next meeting.

He embraced me, and ever so gently He held me close. I looked at Him and said,

> It's hard for me to say goodbye and leave this place. I love You so very much!

As I slowly turned to leave, Yeshua said,

> Wherever you go, Wisdom and Faith will be with you.

CHAPTER 8

HE DELIVERS ME FROM ALL MY FEARS

❀

H E DELIVERS ME from all my fears. I knew that in my heart all so well. Yet somehow it seemed to be one of those times that fear was trying to fill me with stress, as though I were in a pressure cooker. Stress came to me so strong that I just wanted to run away and hide. But the Spirit of Yeshua kept me from running, and I knew that it had to be that I was about to learn something very important in the midst of all this stress. I encouraged myself knowing that what I was going through would not last long. Finally, with joy I hear His voice calling out to me to come to His secret place, His garden of love.

In the midst of all the stress, I ran to Him. Soon I was standing right there before Him, and I expressed to Him,

> It is so good to be here in Your presence, my love. Thank You for Your grace and for having continued to hold me up by Your Spirit. The stress has made me so weary I could hardly keep going!

Then Yeshua replied,

> My beloved, what a joy it is to be here with you. I just want to take a moment to spend time with you and to refresh you. You are such a delight to me, and I enjoy your presence greatly. Let's walk in the garden awhile.

This garden is near Yeshua's palace. The tall trees all around have long overhanging branches and they cover the whole area with shade so that everything is enclosed beneath them. Inside the garden is a bench where we sit. It is framed with white lattice, and there are beautiful pink and lavender flowers that trail up over the top of the frame.

The floor in this part of the garden is large and has flat polished stones that are fitted together to form a patio area. He put His arm around me as we walked through the garden. He led me to the fountain and said,

> Look at all the joy in the water as it splashes and dances out of its source. That is how your innermost being is becoming because of the trials you are going through. You are becoming full of joy, so that each time a trial comes you will be able to truly rejoice in the midst of each trial regardless of how stressful or oppressive it may be. I rejoice in that you have put your trust in Me and have held on to Me and did not cave in to the pressure and run away. Endurance is the most important thing because it will shorten the length of the trial. Praise in the midst of these trials will lift you up above the adverse circumstances.

We walked to the edge of the garden, and we looked out to the surrounding fields of flowers and fields of grain. Yeshua said,

> Look, the fields are white and ready for harvest.

He handed me a small sickle that was very lightweight. And He said,

> It's time for you to go into the harvest field. You will know exactly what to do because you have been preparing for this a long time. Our enemy will not like this; but remember, I am your shield, I am your sword, and I am your secret place. For those who dwell in the secret place with me shall abide under My protection. And I will surely deliver you from the snare of the fowler, as well as the irritating pestilence.
>
> Speak of My abilities over each situation that arises. For I will cover you with the feathers of My protection, and under the safety of My wings you may hide and put your trust, and the truth of My Word shall be your shield and buckler. Then you will not be frightened for the terror that may come by

night, nor the evil words that fly at you by day, nor the pes-
tilence that lurks in darkness, nor the destruction that lays
waste at noonday. For though a thousand should fall at your
side, or ten thousand perish at your right hand, these things
shall not touch you. And with your eyes you shall behold
the reward that is in store for the wicked, because you have
made me, Yeshua, your refuge and your secret place. There-
fore no amount of evil shall be able to overtake you neither
shall any plague come near your dwelling place. I have given
My messengers, the angelic host, charge over you so that you
will not so much as dash your foot against a stone.

Because of your fearlessness and your sense of security
in Me, you will be able to take the authority I have given
you. You will tread over the power of lions, snakes, scor-
pions, and dragons, and trample the enemy under your feet.
Because you have known My name and have set your love
only on Me and have pressed forward into that intimate
secret place with Me, I will always deliver you and set you
high above every trial. All you have to do is call on My
name and I will be quick to answer. The instant I hear you
calling, I will answer you and quickly respond to deliver
you. Then I will lift you up, and honor you, and exalt you
among men. With long life will I satisfy you and show you
the fullness of the joy of My salvation.

After He spoke these things we walked back to the place where
the bench was and we sat down. He put His arms around me and
held me close. I lay my head to rest on His chest. It felt so good just
to relax and rest right there in His arms, no more striving, so more
pushing, no more laboring in my own strength. He lifted my head
and looked me square in the eyes and said,

Remember, the battle is not yours, but Mine. I will go into
the battle and fight for you, for I am your champion war-
rior. I am your Husband, and I will fight for you. All you
have to do is stand on My Word. My Word says,

For God has not given us a spirit of fear, but of power and of love and of a sound mind.

—2 TIMOTHY 1:7

Another important word to stand on:

And we know that all things work together for good to those who love God, to those who are the called according to *His* purpose.

—ROMANS 8:28

And yet another word to stand on:

There is no fear in love [dread does not exist], but full-grown (complete, perfect) love turns fear out of doors and expels every trace of terror! For fear brings with it the thought of punishment, and [so] he who is afraid has not reached the full maturity of love [is not yet grown into love's complete perfection]. We love Him, because He first loved us.

—1 JOHN 4:18–19, AMPC

The most important gift from the Father is love, for faith works by love and it is impossible to please God without faith. Finally, you must praise and worship and exalt My name.

Then Yeshua said,

My beloved, how I love you. You are so special to me, so precious. Your lips are sweet to My taste. Your love is as the fragrance of ointment poured forth. It covers Me and refreshes Me, just your presence is such a delight to Me. I look forward to the next time we meet; and most of all, I look forward to our marriage when we will be together for eternity. I love you and I am so delighted with your progress.

We stood up and I knew it was time to go. Then we said goodbye.

CHAPTER 9

HE IS MY JOY
(THE RIVER OF LIFE)

E IS MY joy. My beloved Savior has called me back again to His mountaintop. It is so wonderful to step into this place. It is the mountain where we had walked before. And I knew He would be there, waiting to meet me.

As I thought on all these past times, His name Yeshua echoed clearly through my heart and mind, and immediately I was there again standing with Him next to the river of life. And He asked me, *"Would you like to have some fun?"*

"Certainly," I answered Him.

"Let's go swimming," He said. As I looked down, I noticed that I was already dressed for swimming, which consisted of a long white top with a gold belt and matching lightweight pants that went down to the ankles. He was wearing practically the same thing. His shirt came down to His hips and He had on long pants.

He said, *"Let's go in."* So we both dove into the water. The water was so cool and refreshing and so wonderful. I swam under the water, up and down, and all around. I was having so much fun and I felt so free. I had never felt so free of all fear or of any hindrances. It felt so free just to flow with the water wherever it went.

Yeshua was right there with me enjoying the water as we flowed right along. He said, *"Let's get out and sit along the bank on the rocks and enjoy the view."* We talked about all the beautiful trees all around us, and then we both became quiet, looking and listening to all our surroundings.

Just then a male and a female deer approached the edge of the water to take a drink. Such a wonderful sight it was; neither of us said a word, just watched. I turned and saw a gorgeous huge water-fall. I asked Him, "Where does it come from?"

And He answered, *"It comes from the Father's throne. Isn't it pow-erful?"* Then I asked Him if we could get closer, and He asked me if I would like to walk under it.

"Oh, could we?" I asked. So we climbed over the rocks and boul-ders at the edge of the waterfall. The noise of it was so loud and the power of it was just awesome. We walked under the waterfall and stood so that the water washed over us. It felt like whatever was filth, or sin, or anything unclean in me began to wash off of my entire being, inside and out. For the first time in my life, I felt so clean. We stood there for a few minutes and enjoyed ourselves. I felt really exhilarated.

Then Yeshua said, *"Let's go."* We walked over by the bank of the river and sat down, and then we both lay down and stared up at the sky. He asked,

Are you ready for this great river to pour out?

"I believe I am. So when will that time come?" I asked.

Soon, it's only a breath away. Hold on a little longer. The river is already flowing, and it will get faster and faster until it will seem like that waterfall flowing down from the Father, and the great harvest will come.

Then Yeshua took me to a higher mountain where we could look down on where we had been. I could see for miles around. I could see that the river was flowing down from a greater mountain. From a distance I could see that the mountain was so high that you couldn't see the top because it was covered in clouds.

Then I said, "What is the name of that mountain?"

Yeshua answered and said,

That's Mt. Zion, the mountain of My Father. As you come up higher, I will take you there. That's the place of His throne and where His glory dwells. When you come up high enough, you can step into heavenly glory.

Again I asked, "When can I go there?"

Yeshua answered, *"Soon, very soon, I will take you there."*

We stood there looking all around us. We could see the people moving below us and then Yeshua came over and put His arm around me and held me close. Yeshua began to sing to me. He had a rich baritone voice that was not really low, but it had a wonderful sound. He sang,

> *My beloved, among others, you are like a lily among thorns. My dove, hiding in the caves high upon the cliff, hidden here on the mountain, let Me see your face, let Me hear your voice. Your voice is sweet, your face is lovely. You are so beautiful, My darling. You are more exciting to Me than any of the other maidens. Your face and neck resemble the Father's favorite mares that are decorated with jewels upon their heads, down the sides of their faces, and down upon their necks. But the decorations that are made for you are a crown of gold with exquisite stones and a silver necklace inlaid with pearls. Your cheeks are so beautiful decorated with gold. Your neck is so beautiful laced with silver.*

Then a song came to me and I sang it to Him, saying,

> *My lover, among the others You are an apple tree among the wild trees in the forest. I enjoy sitting under Your shadow and in Your presence. Your fruit is so sweet to my taste. My lover took me to the wine house; His intent toward me was love. Strengthen me with raisins, refresh me with apples, because I am weak with love. Your left arm is under my head, and Your right arm holds me. I hear Your voice calling to me; here He comes, jumping over the mountains skipping over the hills. You, my lover, are like a gazelle or a young deer leaping over the hills and coming to me.*

Yeshua then sang,

> *Get up, My darling, My beautiful one. Let's go away! Look, winter is past, the rains have come and gone. The flowers are blooming in the fields. It's time to rejoice and sing!*

> *Listen, the doves have returned. Young figs are growing on the fig trees. Smell the air, for the vines are in bloom. Get up, My beloved, My beautiful one. Let's go away!*

When Yeshua finished singing, I sang another song,

> *My lover is mine and I am His. My lover feeds among the lilies, while the day breaks and the shadows run away. Turn my lover, be like a gazelle or a young deer on the mountains of spice and come to me!*

When I finished singing, Yeshua said,

> *What a beautiful song! You have lifted My heart, you have drawn Me closer to you so that I can draw you closer to Me. For I inhabit the praise of My people.*

Then He held me close and wrapped me tighter in His arms and said,

> *I don't want to let you go. I enjoy your presence so much; you bless Me so! Be at peace, My beloved, the winter of your life, the harshness of it is over and spring and new life is on its way. So rejoice! And be glad, for new life is on the horizon.*

Finally He said,

> *But you must go now. I will see you again very soon. I love you.*

What I didn't know at this time was that He would not be leaping and coming to me but I would be coming to Him. I would come to a place where I would be totally surrendered to Him. The Word says, "You are not your own; you were bought at a price" (1 Cor. 6:19–20, NIV). It was Yeshua who paid the high price for me with His life, and I belonged to Him and not myself.

Part 2

ABIDING IN
THE SECRET
PLACE

CHAPTER 10

SPENDING TIME WITH HIM

❧

I HEARD HIM CALL me; and before I knew it, I was in the garden with Him. As we walked I took it all in, reminiscing on the times we had spent together. Everything was just so fresh and alive, even the love we have toward each other. "My beloved, Yeshua, is mine and I am His." We had renewed our covenant. I was taken out of His side. I am bone of His bone and flesh of His flesh. He is everything I need. He put forth His hand of love to me. He embraced me with His right arm.

I hide with Him in His secret place. His garden is my hiding place. His garden was planted with His own hands. He gently and carefully nourishes each and every plant. His garden was filled with every kind of flower as far as the eye can see, in every shade of pink as well as red, gold, and lavender. There all along the sides of the river were trees bearing fruit of apples, pears, and trailing fruit. There was also fruit growing on the vine, bringing to mind again His blood that was shed for me.

Then He led me to our favorite bench where we sat together with white lattice all around us. He held me close and whispered sweet things to me. His love words dripped with milk and honey. He held me close, He kissed me softly, and His sweet breath was like fine perfume to my senses and I breathed in His presence. I know I never want to leave Him. He held me in His arms and His love for me is never ending. He took me to the top of our mountain with His love. There at the top He showed me His universe, how the stars shine and sparkle and how He had called them into their places. He pointed out the planets and showed me how that with the wave of His hand they were all set into their positions.

He is the express image of His Father and all that He knows. It is because He has learned everything from His beloved Father. Even now, I am enraptured in Him. I don't ever want to leave His presence. He is my beloved Savior; and how I love Him, my Yeshua.

After showing me His handiwork, we walked in His garden awhile. A beautiful white horse came up to Him, and began to nuzzle Him, as if he simply wanted to be in His presence also. He mounted the horse and then pulled me up behind Him. We rode down along the mountainside, and there lay before us a beautiful green meadow. As far as the eye can see were fields of flowers. We rode through crocus fields of red and yellow and purple colors. Everything was just so glorious, as though a paintbrush was washed across a canvas. We knew however, that this was a living canvas painted into reality with the Father's brush.

We talked and laughed and I held Him close. I leaned my head against His back as we rode through His creation. Then we came up to another field. This one was all white, a grain field. He pointed out across the field, reminding me,

> *These are all ready for harvesting. The angels have already been sent to thrust in their sickle and stand ready to reap the harvest.*

As we rode I saw just ahead of us an enormous glorious city. All about the Holy City there was a glorious, white glow. He told me that this was the city of God. As we moved closer, I saw people moving toward it. Then He said,

> *People from every tribe, tongue, and nation have come to worship at the throne. Soon I will take you there to see the throne, but not at this time.*

The horse stopped, and then He dismounted. He helped me down, and instantly I lost myself again in His presence. His face radiated with His love for me, and all I could see were His eyes. His eyes were so clear that I could not help but be pulled deep, deep within. My love for Him soared beyond measure. He said to me,

> *I desire the presence of all My beloved children to enjoy walking through the garden with each of them. I want them*

*all to know that I am pleased with them and desire to spend
time with them to show them My love and My ways. They
need to know My ways, for My ways are higher than theirs.
And I have new strategies that they need to know. But to
know these things they need to spend time with Me.*

Then He said,

It's time to go now until our next meeting.

As I turned to leave, He said,

*I love you so deeply, it is all I can do to say goodbye again.
It's getting more difficult to say goodbye each time, because
you please Me so much, and because I delight to be in your
presence. Everything about you pleases Me, and all that
you do in My name is like a sweet fragrance to My senses.
Being in your presence is such a pleasure and it's so precious
to Me. I earnestly anticipate our next meeting. I love you.*

Another time Yeshua called me again into His garden. Oh, how
sweet were the scent of the flowers and the budding of the trees. The
fruit trees were in bloom. The apple and pear blossoms were beautiful to behold and the sweetness of their fragrance was indescribable.

Then He said,

*You are My own private garden prepared only for Me.
Look how I've tended this garden. All the trees are ready
to produce fruit. It's only a matter of time until the fruit
will appear. The blossoms will soon die and the fruit will
take their place. I watch over and closely tend these trees. I
prune the unproductive branches so that everything that is
not good is removed. The things that you have been going
through were My pruning of those unproductive branches.
Now you can see the beautiful result. All of this is going on
in your own heart. Now I just want to encourage you and
refresh you. My call is on your life and that call must be fulfilled. You are My beloved, and oh how I love you. I delight
spending time with you. You are such a joy to Me.*

Yeshua began to sing a song to me,

I am come into My garden, My sister, My spouse. You are My garden, My sister, My spouse. I have gathered My myrrh with My spice, I have eaten My honeycomb with My honey; I have drunk My wine with My milk; eat, O friends, yes, drink abundantly, beloved.

Yeshua continued by saying,

Within your garden contains everything I need. You have set apart for Me the first fruits of My harvest of which no stranger is allowed to partake. Since I am the great High Priest, I receive the first dedicated to Me. Since you belong to Me and everything you have belongs to Me. I have called each garden to be separated for a holy use. Not only what you produce is separated but what you allow to come in should be sanctified for a holy use. I am calling you to greater requirements of separation from the world. Be not conformed to this world, but be ye transformed by the renewal of your mind and heart on the Word of God.

You were destined from the beginning to be molded into My image on the inside. You are the temple of the living God. For what agreement can there be between a temple of God and idols? The Father desires to dwell with man in a temple not made with human hands but a temple made by God Himself. As you are the temple of God, you are also the garden of God, the new Eden, where I might walk with you in the cool of the day. Within this garden you carry the spices of myrrh, which is the fragrant offering of the cross, for you have experienced the death and burial of your old nature and the resurrection of your new nature.

As you have stored up My words in your heart, they are like honey that has been distilled and stored in a honeycomb that I might come and taste and be revived. But these sweet words like honey are also for others that they might be revived.

Then I responded by saying,

Yes, how sweet are Your words to my taste, sweeter than honey to my mouth. More to be desired are they than gold, even than much fine gold. They are sweeter than honey and drippings from the honeycomb. For, my Beloved, You speak pleasant words and they are as a honeycomb sweet to the mind and healing to the body.

Yeshua responded, saying,

For I have eaten of My own words that have distilled within you. They have returned to Me and they are sweeter than honey coming from your mouth to Me and I am refreshed and invigorated. The new wine that has been produced within you is full of life and joy. Remember, I produce My character within you when I come into your garden. Satan comes to steal, kill, and destroy, but I came to bring life, life more abundantly. Therefore, the new wine that's coming forth from you is life with joy unspeakable and full of glory. Since you have taken in the milk of the Word you have much stored within, therefore, you are able to feed others what you have taken in. This milk is to feed the babes, My new ones. I am very encouraged by your progress for you are able to feed the little ones."

Yeshua began to sing another song over me,

Behold, thou art fair, My love; behold, thou art fair. Thou hast dove's eyes within thy locks; thy hair is a flock of goats that appear from mount Gilead.

Yeshua continued by saying,

I am now beginning to see Myself in you. In My Father's Word it says that we all, with open face beholding as in a mirror the glory of the Lord, are changed into the same image from glory to glory, even as by the Spirit of the Lord, the glory of the only begotten Son. Now I can see your true beauty, for your dove's eyes are focused completely on Me and you are able to see with My eyes the things of the Spirit.

You have surrendered your life to the work of the Holy Spirit within you and are seeing the things of the Spirit. Therefore, you are set apart for the Lord's use. Your hair speaks again of that life that has been set apart for the Father's use; a holy vessel for God's holy use.

When Yeshua finished speaking, He kissed me on the forehead and said,

You are such a blessing to Me!

Then Yeshua put His arms around me and held me close. I could feel His strength and power going into me. It was like cool refreshing water flowing into me after walking through a hot dry desert.

As He held me, I closed my eyes, and I felt His warmth and His love. The sweet fragrance of cinnamon and myrrh wafted gently past my senses, and I know I didn't want to let go of Him. My Yeshua is my Beloved. Finally He said,

It won't be much longer. The fruit is coming soon. I'm pouring out My Spirit so that all will know who I am.

Again He held me tight and said,

I don't want to let you go, but I must. It's getting late.

Then I said,

I love You so much. You are my strength, my shield and my high tower. You have truly made me an eagle to soar higher and higher above the circumstances. You are everything I need. Thank You for keeping me for such a time as this. I love You so much. Thank You for calling me again and again to be in Your presence. I will wait with anticipation for our next meeting. I Love You.

Another time Yeshua called me and before I knew it I was sitting next to my Adonai. We were in the heavenlies above the earth, because my Lord Yeshua is enthroned in our praises. Then Yeshua said, "*Would you like to have some fun?*"

I responded by saying, "Yes!"

As I sat at His side, taking what looked like a glowing ball in His right hand, He said, "*Look what happens as I throw this ball of fire to the earth.*" Yeshua took the ball of fire and threw it to the earth into the midst of the people and when it hit the people their faces lit up with the glory of God.

Yeshua then threw another ball of fire and again the people's faces lit up with the glory of God. Then He handed me one of the balls and said, "*Here, you can send one down too.*" I took the ball and threw it down and the same thing happened—the people's faces lit up with the glory of God. He gave me two more balls and they did the same thing.

Finally Yeshua said,

> The knowledge of the glory of the Lord shall cover the earth as the waters cover the sea. My Word also says in Isaiah 60 to arise and shine and be radiant with the glory of the Lord, for your light has come, and the glory of the Lord has risen upon you.

Then Yeshua said,

> Gross darkness shall cover the earth; but don't be afraid, because the light of My glory shall cover you. My glory will be like the sun shining on a mirror that will blind the enemy. I will make you that ball of fire that I will cast in the midst of the people of the earth. I have anointed you to carry My glory. So be of good cheer, I have overcome the world.

CHAPTER 11

THE THRONE ROOM

_~᎒᎒_

HEARD MY BELOVED Savior call me, and before I knew it, I was standing in His beautiful garden. My Yeshua was there to meet me with outstretched arms and a kiss. I gazed around the garden and saw all the beautiful things He had given life to. In His embrace I also received much needed refreshment from all the life that came from Him as He held me close. Then He said,

> _I have brought you here to show you more of My kingdom._
> _I would like to take you to My Father's throne room and_
> _show you of things to come._

We walked through the garden and I saw flowering trees knowing that fruit would soon be on them. After we left the garden, we walked out on to the edge of a valley. Yeshua said,

> _This valley looks like a valley on earth where the last great_
> _battle will take place between the kingdom of My Father_
> _and the kingdom of darkness and our enemy Satan. This_
> _is to let you know that no matter how dark things seem to_
> _get that I will win the victory for all mankind. The earth_
> _belongs to Me, and everything in it. All those who follow_
> _Me will reign on the earth with Me._

We stood there looking down at the valley from our high vantage point for a moment, and I could breathe in the fresh cool air and tried to imagine what it would be like. I asked Him, "What will it be like?" Then He said,

> _All the kings of the earth will rise up against My chosen_
> _people, Yishrael, and they will come and fight here, but I_

*will come and redeem My people just like it was spoken of
in My Word.*

As we walked, I noticed vineyards all along the way. Then I heard
Yeshua say,

*The vineyards have produced much fruit and they are ripe
for the harvest and soon there will be new wine.*

We continued to walk on and came to a stable where horses were
being groomed and taken care of. The most interesting part was that
all the horses were white.

One of the horses came over and nuzzled Him. Yeshua reached
up, patted the horse's neck and then stroked his head. Yeshua
motioned to me to come and said, *"Let's go riding."*

He brought another horse for me to ride. It had been a long time
since I had ridden a horse, but once I got on I felt as if I had been
riding horses all along. Then Yeshua said,

Just follow Me!

We rode out through the meadows where I saw people in the
fields harvesting grain. They were binding up the grain in bundles
and stacking them up. Then Yeshua said,

*Those bundles will be taken to the threshing floor where
they will be beaten and the grain kernels and chaff will be
separated. So it will be the same in the kingdom. The grain
will be used either for bread or it will be planted as seed to
produce thirty, sixty, a hundredfold return and the chaff
will be burned.*

As we rode, I could see other fields ready for harvest. We came to
a river, the river of life, and Yeshua said,

We must cross this river before we can go on.

He guided His horse to step into the river and I followed. As we
got into the deeper water, I began to laugh. I laughed and laughed
until I couldn't stay on my horse and I fell back into the water. I felt
so exhilarated, as though I were drunk. I just lay there in the water

laughing and laughing. Even Yeshua threw His head back laughing. Then He said,

> It's the river of life. It brings such cleansing joy. The joy of the Lord is your strength. You will need physical and spiritual strength where we are going.

Finally, Yeshua got down and picked me up and gave me a hug and a kiss and put me back on the horse; or I would have stayed there forever. Yeshua then told me,

> You will have all eternity to come back and visit this place. We must be moving on.

After leaving the river we rode up over a ridge and I saw it. The city of my Lord stretched out into the horizon. It went so far that it looked like it had no ending. It was the heavenly Yerusalem. There was such a glow on the Holy City. The walls sparkled with a radiant light; and like rain falling with the sunlight shining through, there were little rainbows shining out everywhere I looked. Then Yeshua said, "Let us go in."

My eyes could hardly take in all the beauty. The streets were made of what looked like gold, but it was transparent for you could see through it. As we rode through the gate called Beautiful, I could see it was truly beautiful everywhere I looked. We dismounted from our horses. Yeshua took my hand and said, "Let us go this way."

In the distance I could hear bagpipes playing a beautiful rendition of "Amazing Grace." I thought to myself, "God's grace is truly amazing!" Yeshua must have read my thoughts, because He said,

> Yes, God's grace is amazing.

It was like walking through the streets of the earthly Yerusalem with the stone walls and the big arches over the streets, except this time the stones were made of precious stones. The walls were opal, and inlayed around the arches over the doors were amethyst and emerald. Everything was so beautiful!

Some of the people were walking along the streets and some of the people were gathered in clusters laughing and talking. When we walked by, everyone stopped and touched Him. I guess I didn't really understand who He was until then.

We kept walking until we came to an enormous building with great columns around the outside. People were coming in and going out constantly. As we came near the courtyard, Yeshua said,

This is the outer court where the sacrifices are made.

In the outer court we passed the altar of sacrifice. It was made of bronze, and coals of fire were burning underneath the grate. Yeshua said,

This represents your life of sacrifice. Even when you are in the fiery trials of life and you continue to serve the Lord, your life is a sweet smelling savor to the Lord My Father. My Word says to buy from Me gold tried by fire.

We continued on until we came to a large bronze basin full of water. Yeshua again explained by saying,

This laver represents God's unending mercy, that when you have gone through the fire there is the washing and cleansing power of the Father's Word and His forgiveness.

After Yeshua explained about the altar and the laver, I replied,

Now I understand a little more about the Father's kingdom.

Then we moved on toward two enormous doors that were hand carved from olive wood. Once we stepped inside I saw a large open space. The floor was of large pieces of emerald and amethyst. The ceiling seemed to be at least forty feet in height with gold around the edges.

As I stood there, I felt such love. As I got closer to the throne room, I felt the love of the Father intensify. I was so overwhelmed that I began to weep. I fell to the floor and wept and wept. Yeshua stooped down, put His arms around me and held me close until I stopped crying. He said,

Now you know where the love comes from and how I was able to go through the Cross. I did it because of the love of

*My Father. I spent so much time with Him that His love
for Me enabled Me to finish the Cross. It was His loving
grace that strengthened Me. Now I sit with Him at His
right hand.*

Yeshua paused as if in thought and said, *"Let us continue on."*

On the other side of the room were more marble pillars and as
we walked past them I saw two more hand carved olive wood doors.
Once past these doors Yeshua took my hand and began to show
and explain to me the holy articles that were in the holy place. He
started by saying,

*On our left is the golden candlestick with the seven branches
lighted continually with never ending oil. This lamp represents the sevenfold Spirit of God in every believer and the
oil represents the infilling of the Holy Spirit.*

Then He pointed to the right and said,

*This is the golden table of show bread with the twelve loaves
of unleavened bread which represents the continual taking
in of the Word of My Father. And finally straight ahead
is the golden altar of incense which represents the sweet
prayers of the saints.*

As we pressed past the altar of incense, I could see the brightness and the glory of the Father coming from the holy place. At the
entrance to the holy place were two huge gold doors guarded by two
giant angelic guards with great golden shields. They stood on either
side of the doors and they opened the doors as we passed through.

When we walked into the holy place, the place of the Father's
throne, I felt so dirty and unclean that all I could do was fall on my
face and cry out for mercy. The Father's holiness was so great that I
felt totally undone and speechless. Yeshua said,

*Remember the blood of the Lamb; remember the blood of
the Lamb.*

When I raised myself up and looked at my hands I saw that they were clean and my clothes were white as snow without spot or wrinkle. Yeshua reminded me,

> *You have free access into the throne room of God through the blood of the Lamb. Remember, I am the great High Priest who is passed into the heavens—Yeshua, the Son of God. For I was in all points tempted just like you, yet I was without sin. And as it is written,*

> Let us therefore come boldly to the throne of grace, that we may obtain mercy and find grace in time of need.
> —HEBREWS 4:16

I am a priest forever after the order of Melchizedek.

After Yeshua said this, I began to look around the room. I saw people smiling and praising the Lord of glory for the great things He had done. I heard the cherubim and the seraphim crying, "Holy, holy, holy, to the Lord God Almighty who was, who is, and who is to come and to the Lamb upon the throne." There were people from every tribe and nation and tongue giving glory to the Father. This multitude was singing songs of praise, with joy and abandonment to the music.

In front there were ladies all dressed in white garments singing, dancing, and playing tambourines. The tambourines had red, yellow, pink, and green ribbons streaming down. These same colored ribbons were in their hair and tied around their waists.

Following the dancers were men carrying seven banners all sewn in brilliant colors. The banners were King of Kings and Lord of Lords, The Lamb of God, Savior of the World, Everlasting Father, Prince of Peace, Lion of Judah, and The Great I Am. They were of brilliant colors of red, gold, blue, and purple. As the banners passed by the glory cloud filled the room so that you could hardly stand.

The music began to slow down and the songs began to worship the Lord of glory. I saw so many people standing with eyes closed and hands lifted high. Some were down on their knees and some were lying out on the floor totally worshiping the Lord.

People from every tongue, tribe, and nation were singing in unity "Great Is Thy Faithfulness," and then they sang "Holy, holy, holy." I became completely lost in the worship. When I finally opened my eyes, I saw Yeshua seated on His throne in all the glory of His Father. In fact when I looked at Yeshua I could see the Father glorified all around Him. When Yeshua turned His head to the right or to the left, I could see the Father.

Yeshua was dressed in a long robe with a golden sash tied around His chest. His head and hair were white like wool; wool that is white as snow. His eyes were flames of fire. His feet were like brass that glows hot in a furnace. His voice was like the noise of flooding waters as He spoke up and said,

> I'm calling all My warriors together for the final battle. I'm joining you in prayer to birth the final move to bring the kingdom of My Father into its fullness. Each one of you must seek Me in prayer for the wisdom to overcome in these last hours.

Everyone said, "Holy, holy, holy to the Lamb upon the throne." Then the music started up again, and I closed my eyes and sang, "Holy, holy, holy," with everyone. They sang "To Him Who Sits on the Throne," and I became lost in the glory.

When I opened my eyes, Yeshua was standing there beside me again. I felt His love for me again and I began to weep. He held me in His arms until the tears subsided. I saw all the people and I remembered what He had said. Then I said, "What did you mean when you were talking about birthing the kingdom?"

Yeshua replied,

> In order to bring the finality of My Father's kingdom into being, it will take much prayer and much pain. Just like a woman has much pain in labor to bring forth a child into the world, so we must also. There must be great bearing down and pressing in, just like the woman begins to bear down. Once the labor has begun, it will not stop until the child is birthed. There will be the beginnings of persecution in your world, so I wanted to let you know so you would

be aware; but remember, you are not to depend on your
own wisdom or own ability. You are to call on Me and
depend on My strength. Remember, the joy of the Lord is
your strength.

Then He explained,

When you are praising My Father on the earth, you may be
on the earth in your body but you are really in the holy of
holies. The people you saw are other believers just like you
who have come to worship in the heavenlies.

We made our way out of the throne room and Yeshua said, "*Come*
with Me, I want to show you My palace."

We walked out through the marble pillars to the courtyard of the
temple and walked down a stone pathway and through the garden
gate. There was a trellis on the right side with pink flowers blooming
profusely and the sweet smell of gardenias floated in the air.

Yeshua led me across an open porch and through a door that
was of intricately cut leaded glass that reflected all the colors of the
rainbow. He had brought me into His own personal palace. There
was a beautiful tapestry on the wall of white horses running in a
meadow. The floor was of polished wood, and there was a beautiful
woven rug in the center of the room. There was a fireplace with black
granite around the opening, and natural stone made up the hearth.
Next to the fireplace there was an enormous overstuffed armchair.
As we came closer to the fireplace, I noticed a square glass-topped
table with a carafe of water and a bowl of assorted fruit in it.

Yeshua said,

Here are some pillows we can sit on and sit in front of the
fire and rest and get refreshed.

Then He gave me a glass of cool water and we both ate some of
the fruit. We lay back and propped ourselves on two large pillows
and stared into the fire without saying a word, just remembering the
day and enjoying each other's company. After awhile Yeshua looked
at me and said,

Thank you for being patient and long-suffering and waiting with Me. There are so many people who are bound up in their minds, and it takes patience and perseverance and prayer to set them free. Remember, when you pray I do hear you; and when those prayers are in agreement with My Father's Word, I will answer them.

Then He said,

There is much to do in the kingdom to get prepared for these last days. Each one must sanctify himself and set himself aside for the Master's use. We must be willing and obedient vessels fit for My Father's use. The trials that you went through were in preparation for such a time as this.

I said, "What must I do to be prepared?"
Yeshua answered,

You must put My Father's Word deep within you. Then you must pray and speak the Word and fast. Finally, you must not forget to praise and to worship My Father and to be continually thankful in every situation.

Then I replied,

Thank you so much for telling me all these things. I know I must have your help, wisdom and strength, in order to accomplish any of the things you spoke of. My Yeshua, I love you so much. You are so full of mercy and grace.

He put His arm around me and held me close. Thinking we might be leaving soon, I said, "Yeshua I don't want to leave you," and I put my head against His chest and held Him tight.

We sat there together for awhile without saying anything and then I heard the music. The music had a long slow beat and a sort of Middle Eastern flair. It started out slow but it began to beat faster and faster. Yeshua was moved by it until He said, *"Would you like to dance?"*

I got up and said, "Yes."

He took both of my hands and we began to sway to the left and then to the right. He put one hand at my waist and we took a step to the left and one to the right, and then we turned and went the other way. The music went faster and faster and we laughed and laughed until it slowed down. Then Yeshua stopped.

As a new song began to play, I raised my hands, closed my eyes, and began to sway back and forth. Before I knew it, I was dancing before my King. Across one of the tables, there was a gold shawl with long fringe hanging from it and I took it and put it across my shoulders. I danced and danced slowly before my Lord.

As I danced, I could see His eyes as they poured out His love for me and all the love I had for Him came pouring forth in rivers of love and worship for Him. I poured out my life before Him until I fell weeping at His feet.

Yeshua pulled me into His arms and said, *"Thank you for blessing Me with your love and your passionate heart."*

He looked deep into my eyes and said, *"I love you so much,"* and then held me close again.

Yeshua finally said, *"You know we need to be going back."*

After a moment of silence I answered, "Yes, I know."

Yeshua led me out the same way we came in. Along the way, I noticed a beautiful white two-tiered fountain made out of a pearlescent marble. As the light shined through the falling water, it looked like sparkling diamonds.

We continued walking until we were out on the street again. Someone brought the horses to us and helped me mount my horse.

"This whole experience has been a healing time for me," I thought to myself.

Then Yeshua said, *"I'm going to take you back a different way this time, so follow Me closely."*

We rode our horses out across a meadow full of yellow and pink flowers. As we rode side by side, Yeshua said,

> *You know there will be persecution and some people will die*
> *for the kingdom of My Father as it is brought to the earth.*
> *For the kingdom suffers violence and the violent ones take*
> *it by force.*

I agreed with Him and said, "Deep down in my heart I have always known this."

As we rode I could see we were entering a forest. I saw a little cottage nestled among the trees. Yeshua said, *"Since it's getting late we will rest in this cottage for the night and start out again in the morning."*

It was a beautiful little cottage. It had a thatched roof and natural stone on the outside. When we walked in the door, I could see that there was a stone fireplace and the floor was a dark stained polished wood. We found some blankets in a closet and there was plenty of food in the pantry, as though someone knew we were coming. Yeshua put some wood on the fire, and we gathered our blankets on the floor to sit in front of the fire and rest. I was so weary that all I wanted to do was sleep and that I did.

Suddenly, with a jolt I was awakened from a sound sleep and I found that I was alone. I was trying to figure out why I was awakened, and then I heard a bang at the door. I stood up and looked around for Yeshua but He wasn't there. Then the door flew open, and in the firelight I could see a massive horrendous form. It was so horrible that it was indescribable. I couldn't describe it because it kept changing its form. The whole room filled up with the presence of terror. That stench of evil seemed to envelope me and tried to overtake me but a peaceful still small voice rose up on the inside and I said,

> *God has not given me a spirit of fear, but of power and of love and of a sound mind. Of power because My Father has given me power to tread on serpents and scorpions and over all the power of the enemy and nothing shall by any means hurt me. Of love, because Yeshua has loved me with an everlasting love and with loving-kindness He has drawn me. He said He would never leave me nor forsake me. And of a sound mind, because I have the mind of Yeshua and do hold the thoughts, intents, and purposes of My Father's own heart.*

When I spoke these words out loud that whole presence of terror disintegrated. Then I felt a presence behind me. When I turned around, it was Yeshua. "Where were You?" I asked.

He answered,

I was and Am within you, for I am omnipresent.

I responded, "Oh, thank You!" Light then began to stream into the little cottage as the sun came up.

I asked, "What was that?"

Yeshua answered,

> *That was the spirit of terrorism that the enemy is trying to send across the land. My children must stand firm against it. This will be a great teaching and revelation for those who will rule with Me. The psalms in My Book will have new meaning for My people. Now you will really know how to use My Word, overcome with its authority and rule over the evil in this world. You will begin to see the manifestation of the power of My Word to overthrow anything it is sent against. I and My Word are one, and I have been given all authority by My Father over all things in heaven, earth, and below the earth. At My name, Yeshua, every knee must bow and every tongue confess that Yeshua Messiah, the Savior of the world, is Lord, to the glory of My Father in heaven.*

After this He said, "Here, I have some fruit, bread, and water for you to be refreshed."

We sat on the floor and ate and drank. Finally we picked up everything and put it away for the next sojourner who would pass this way.

Then Yeshua said, "Would you like to ride with Me for awhile since you were up awhile during the night? You can rest as we ride."

So He helped me up on the horse. I sat in front and He sat behind me and put His arms around me and held me close. I closed my eyes and rested and was at peace in His loving and protecting arms. After resting in His arms I woke up to a beautiful cool morning. Then He stopped the horses and we got off for some refreshing cool water. Yeshua asked, "Would you like to ride on your horse for awhile?"

I answered, "Yes." So I mounted my horse and we rode side by side. I thought we must be coming close to the stables because things began to look familiar.

Yeshua said, "*Let's race!*"

I responded, "*Yes, let's race!*"

We started running our horses. First He would get ahead, and then I would get ahead. The exhilaration of running the horses was wonderful. The wind was blowing through my hair and there was such joy. The joy was the result of the freedom that I felt. All the bondages of the past were gone and all those things that had so easily beset me had been put off. I was running the race without hindrances. We were coming to the finish line, and Yeshua was beside me as we finished the race.

I lifted up my hands and as the wind blew past my face and through my hair I knew that "I WAS FREE AT LAST!"

When we arrived at the stables there were people there to meet us. We dismounted and they took the horses to cool them down, groom them, and give them water and feed.

We walked from the stables through the same area that we came through the first time until we came to the vineyards. I knew there was a teaching here from Him. Finally I asked Him, "What do You mean by 'new wine'?"

> *If you will abide in Me, hide My words in your heart, and spend time with Me, I will pour into you new life. As the old lifestyle is given up and you allow Me to fill you up with new life through My Spirit, then it will be like pouring in new wine. First the grapes have to be picked and then crushed, like the old nature. The crushing of the grapes is giving up your rights to do things your own way. As your will and old ways are crushed and done away with, then I can flow through you in an unhindered way. I am sanctifying you completely through and through. Then I can truly use you as My warrior and show you My plans to bring My kingdom to earth. It will take great mighty warriors— warriors of renown, warriors that have proved My Word. For My Word is true. As soldiers go through boot camp and are toughened through rigorous training, so are My people being prepared. They will depend on My voice and My Word and not on their emotions. The juice is then put*

in a new vessel to ferment, which gives it a new form of life.
Thus new wine, just like sweet new wine, your life abiding
in Me is sweet abundant life.

We then continued walking back toward the garden again. I kept remembering our time in the holy place and what He said to me about the pain of the labor beginning and it wouldn't stop until there was a birth. I wondered what kind of pain we would be facing.

Then Yeshua said,

> *There will be tribulations and persecutions and some will*
> *die for the kingdom of My Father. Just as it was in the past,*
> *so will it be again. My Word says that in the world you will*
> *have trials and tribulations; but be of good cheer, for I have*
> *overcome the world.*

We walked back into the garden through the garden gate and I saw the bubbling fountain of joy and all the beautiful flowers and the fruit trees. It was good to be back in the garden again, but I knew it must be time to go back. We sat on our favorite bench under the grape arbor with the flowers trailing down, but we didn't say much at first. Then Yeshua pulled me close and put His arm around me and said,

> *I just want you to tell My people how much I love them and*
> *especially to tell them I am in the midst of their lives and*
> *that they are not alone in this war we are fighting. I am the*
> *Prince of the Lord's host. I am the great warrior King and*
> *I am the Lion of the Tribe of Judah and the battle is Mine.*
> *I will go before you and prepare the way and I will make a*
> *way for you where there seems to be no way.*

Then I lay my head on His chest and closed my eyes and rested. I don't know how long I rested there, but Yeshua said, "*I thank you for your worship and your songs for they bless Me so.*"

I replied, "You are so worthy of all of my worship because I love You so much."

He hugged me and said, *"It's not much longer and we will be together for eternity."*

I knew then that it was time for me to go. We stood up and one of His messengers was there to escort me home.

Yeshua gave me one last embrace and held me close for a long time as though He knew I would be going through some things. I held on too, for I knew He was my strength and my song.

CHAPTER 12

HOLY GROUND AND HIGH PLACES

⟨⟨⟨⟨⟩⟩⟩⟩

HEARD YESHUA MY Savior's words as He pulled me up to the top of the mountain.

It's time to come up to a new vantage point.

As I stood at the edge of the mountain, I took a deep breath and inhaled the cool refreshing air. There were no birds in the air and no sounds being made, only peace and quiet. All I could hear was the wind blowing through my hair.

As I looked around, I could see that we were on the highest point of all the mountains. I could see the tops of the other mountains all around me. When I looked down I could see valleys and even a river cut out of the rocks below.

Yeshua knew what I was thinking because He said,

> *From this high vantage point, you can see our enemy on the move. He cannot hide his schemes from us. I have brought you to this place to instruct you about sitting at My right hand in heavenly places. Because I went to the cross and then went into hell, I took the keys of hell and death from Satan our enemy and arose to sit at My Father's right hand. My Father in heaven gave all authority over to Me. When you use My name, behold I give you power and authority to trample on all the power the enemy possesses. This power and authority includes physical and mental strength and ability over Satan and his schemes. Therefore nothing shall, by any means, hurt you.*

I said,

> I know I must believe all of this by faith.

Yeshua replied,

> Yes, because spiritual power and authority that I give you is
> not what you can see with your natural eyes. Having spiri-
> tual authority is something that must be seen with the eyes
> of faith by the power of the Holy Spirit.

Then Yeshua went on to say,

> Our enemy dwells in high places even on mountains. Our
> enemy is the accuser of the brethren. He will use man to
> speak evil and to speak curses over My people. But what
> God has blessed, man or Satan cannot curse. My Father
> has given us power to speak blessings over our fellow man.
> He has also given us power to speak destruction over our
> enemy Satan and his demonic horde.

Questioning Him I said,

> You mean I have the authority and power to speak destruc-
> tion to the enemy Satan's plans and schemes?

Yeshua answered,

> Yes, you do, when you abide in Me and My words abide in
> you. My Word says of Yishrael,

> God brings them out of Egypt; He has strength like a wild
> ox; He shall consume the nations, his enemies; He shall
> break their bones And pierce them with his arrows.
>
> —NUMBERS 24:8

> When you speak My promises, they are swords and arrows
> against our enemy, Satan's hordes, crushing their bones and
> piercing them through.

Yeshua continued,

The high places enable us to behold the other believers and where they are in My kingdom so that you may know how to pray for them and speak My promises and blessings over them. Blessed of God is he who blesses you, who prays for and contributes to your welfare.

Not quite understanding what He was saying, I asked,

How can I get to holy ground or to the high places?

Yeshua answered, saying,

In order to go to the high places, you must first be on holy ground. When you are on holy ground, you are in the presence of My Father.

Yeshua thought a moment and said,

You come to holy ground through the power of the Holy Spirit in the way of prayer, fasting, or worship. When spending time on holy ground, you will hear the words of My Father. Having your eyes opened and uncovered, you will see a true vision of My Father and know who He really is. Not only will you see a vision of My Father and your eyes be opened, but My Father will reveal to you the future things to come. While standing on holy ground you will receive wisdom from My Father for every situation in your life, whether great or small. Most of all you will realize that miracles come from the Father. Here you will see the Father at work healing and making people whole. The Father will reveal His fullness as the Creator of all things. When you have spent enough time with the Father, then He will show you the high places where the battle with our adversary is being fought. When you speak the Father's promises, His holy angels go forth and war against the enemy. The Father's Word says we win. In the high places the main weapons the enemy uses are fear and deception.

I asked,

What are we to do in high places?

Yeshua replied by saying,

Your main goal is to possess the land that our enemy has stolen. Possess the land and take back the people and the spoils that belong to us. My Father says in His Word,

You shall drive out all the inhabitants of the land before you and destroy all their figured stones and destroy all their figured stones and all their molten images and completely demolish all their [idolatrous] high places. And you shall take possession of the land and dwell in it, for to you I have given the land to possess it.

—NUMBERS 33:52–53, AMPC

There is none like My Father who rides through the heavens to your help and His majestic glory through the skies. My Father is your refuge and dwelling place and underneath are the everlasting arms. He will drive the enemy before you and thrust them out, saying, Destroy! My Father will daily give His plans and strategies, and if you will listen diligently to His voice, being watchful to do all He asks, then He will set you high above all the nations of the earth. As an eagle that stirs up her nest, that flutters over her young, My Father will spread abroad His wings and He will bear you on His pinions. He will make you ride on the high places of the earth. In the high places you will ride above your trials and your pain.

Then Yeshua looked into my face and asked me if I was ready to be a watchman on the high places. I said,

My Yeshua, only You know the answer. For I know that I can't do anything in my own strength. I must have Your grace.

Just as I finished speaking, one of Yeshua's heavenly chariots pulled up beside the mountain and we stepped inside. In the interior of the chariot there were two seats facing each other and a window on either side. We sat facing one another. Yeshua began to tell me of the importance of being a watchman on the high places.

When you have spent time with My Father on holy ground, then My Father will put you in high places as a watchman for His kingdom. As a watchman you will pray in the Spirit in every season with all manner of prayer and entreaty for all believers everywhere. My Father will reveal to you the truth and He will ask you to speak His words to others to encourage the faint of heart and to lift up those that have no might. If you see the sword come upon the land, you will blow the trumpet and warn the people. But if you see the sword come and do not blow the trumpet and the people are not warned, if the sword comes and takes any person from among them, he is taken away in his iniquity; but his blood I will require at the watchman's hand. So I have set thee, a watchman, over My house; therefore you shall hear the word at My mouth, and warn them for Me. When I say to the wicked, "Thou shall surely die," and you do not give him a warning or speak to warn the wicked from his wicked way, to save his life, the same wicked man shall die in his iniquity; but his blood I shall require at your hand. Yet, if you warn the wicked and he does not turn from his wickedness or from his wicked way, he shall die in his iniquity; but you have delivered your soul.

Then Yeshua said,

You shall declare the good tidings of the gospel of peace. You shall shout with joy salvation. You will say to others, "Our God reigns." You shall not stop proclaiming and making mention that Yeshua Messiah is King. You shall bring others up the mountain to bring them into the presence of My Father. Finally, you will hear the voice of My Father. To know the Father's plans against our enemy, so

ambushments can be set up against him. Together we will
destroy and bring to nothing every plan and scheme our
enemy has.

As Yeshua talked, my thoughts went over every detail of His
teachings. I wanted to remember everything He said. Of course He
knew my thoughts because He said,

My Holy Spirit will bring back to you everything I have
said.

We both sat back in our seats; and then He moved over and sat
beside me. He put His arm across my shoulders and drew me close
to Him.

I said,

Yeshua, all that You have said seems so overwhelming to
me; so much responsibility. It's more than I can take in.

Yeshua replied,

My Holy Spirit will be your instructor and your guide. He
will help you in every area to be My Father's vessel. Just
lean on Him and not rely on yourself or your own wisdom.

Yeshua held me in His arms awhile so that I could rest and be
refreshed. Then He said, "*It's time for you to go back down the moun-*
tain until our next meeting. I love you."

CHAPTER 13

STRONGHOLDS

꩜

MY SAVIOR CALLED me to His garden. And as He took my hand, I heard Him say the word "strongholds." I thought to myself, "What does He mean by strongholds?"

Yeshua answered by saying,

> I have brought you here to teach you about the hiding places of our enemy. Our enemy is a liar and the father of lies. He does not know how to tell the truth. Everything he has taken he has taken by flattery, scheming, deception, half-truths, and lies. Our enemy steals, kills, and destroys; but I have come that you might have life. My children have already given him so much land because of ignorance. As children of My Father, our main goal is to possess the land that originally belonged to My Father. Out of ignorance of My Father's truths, My children have let the enemy steal, kill, and destroy what was rightfully their inheritance— their souls.

I asked Yeshua,

> What must I do to take back what belongs to me?

Yeshua replied,

> You must know the truth of My Father's Word and know how to use this truth as a weapon against our enemy to take back the land. There are so many people who are wounded, battered, and bruised by words spoken over them and against them. There are people whose minds are kept in darkness. They are held in captivity and bondage to the

lies of the enemy. But My Father and I have come to set the captives free. Our enemy will speak words to people that are lies and bring destruction. The enemy will use these lies to build a fortress. When the people believe these lies, then the fortress becomes a stronghold. When someone tells you, "You can't do that," and you believe what they say, then you have allowed a stronghold to be built.

I replied,

What must I do to tear these strongholds down?

Yeshua answered,

You must use My Father's words of truth which say,

I can do all things through [Yeshua] who strengthens me.
—PHILIPPIANS 4:13

When you keep speaking this truth over again to yourself and believe it, the stronghold of that lie will come down. My Father's words of truth are like a battering ram being used against the gate of a huge fortress. You must hit the gate again and again without stopping until the gate is totally demolished. Then you must go in and destroy the forces of darkness with the truth. If there is sickness, then there must be words about healing. But you must believe My Father's promises. Remember that I was beaten and crucified, and by those stripes you were healed.

Yeshua added by saying,

Another type of stronghold is the sin and selfishness of man. That sin is pride. One of the strongest and most difficult strongholds to pull down is pride. The truth for this stronghold is to worship the Lord your God, and serve Him only. My Father will bring down that pride and humility will come forth by allowing trials and tribulations. The truth for that is to trust in the Lord with all your heart and lean not on your own understanding. Acknowledge Him in all your ways and

*He will direct your path. One of the many areas of strongholds
is the selfishness of man. Just as our enemy, Satan uses flat-
tery, scheming, deception, half-truths, and lies, sin-controlled
men use these same methods to get what they want. In order
to walk in truth you must first seek the Father's will for every
situation. You must ask for the Father's plans and direction
because if it's the Father's will, the Father will go before you
and make a way. Therefore, you won't have to use Satan's
methods in your life. When you have done something wrong,
come to Me and ask Me to show you what to do to correct it.
Don't try to cover up, but tell the truth. Just come to Me and
I will show you the way of truth.*

*The most important truth you must know is that I and
My Father love you. You are loved with an everlasting love
and with lovingkindness we have drawn you. The love of
My Father is the greatest power in the heavens, in the earth,
and under the earth. My Word says,*

Neither death nor life, nor angels nor principalities nor
powers, nor things present nor things to come, nor height
nor depth, nor any other created thing, shall be able to separate us from the love of God, which is in [Me].

—ROMANS 8:38–39

*The Father is your strength and your hiding place, your
stronghold in times of trouble. My Father knows those who
trust and take refuge in Him. He is your strength and fortress and your refuge in the day of affliction."*

I replied,

*Thank You for loving me and keeping me through every
trial. Where would I go if I didn't have Your love?*

Yeshua put His arms around me and held me close to His chest
and said,

*I love you so much and I am very pleased with your prog-
ress. You are allowing Me to be Lord over every area of
your life, even your thought life.*

Yeshua added,

*There is another stronghold that must come down. That
stronghold is idolatry and false religion, the worship of
anyone or anything other than the Father, Son and the
Holy Spirit. When you have seen Me, you've seen the
Father. When you have the Holy Spirit you have the Father.
We are all one. The Word says, Worship the Lord your
God and Him only will you serve. There are so many false
religions in the world, but only I have come to save and forgive. I came that you might have life and have it abundantly.
I came to redeem mankind and restore his broken relationship back to the Father. I am the kinsman Redeemer, but
I will not share My glory with any man. I will not allow
witchcraft, soothsayers, or sorcery, nor will I allow the worship of idols. Idolatry includes the worship of self, other
people, and animals, for I am a jealous God. These are an
abomination to Me.*

Lastly Yeshua said,

*Fear is the final stronghold that I want to teach you about
at this time. Fear is the major weapon the enemy uses
against My children. The truth is that the Father has not
given you a spirit of fear, but of power and love and a
sound mind. My Father is a loving Father whose thoughts
towards you are good and not evil and that we would have
a good end. The Father wants to bless you with good things.
The truth that will destroy fear is that you are loved with
an everlasting love and with loving kindness the Father has
drawn you. I have promised that I will never leave you
nor forsake you. Fear not, for I will go before you and prepare the way. I will change and soften hearts before you
get there. Remember, My Father is your strength, your fortress, and your refuge in the day of affliction. He is your*

protector and redeemer from the evil one. The Father has given you the strength and power to tread on serpents and scorpions and all the power of the enemy; there is nothing that can hurt you. My God has not given you a spirit of fear, but of power and love and a sound mind. You have the mind of Christ and do hold the thoughts, intents, and purposes of God's own heart. Finally, whatever things are true, honest, just, pure, lovely, and of good report, with virtue and praise, think on these things.

I responded by speaking the Word back to my Beloved,

*I will love You, O L*ORD*, my strength. The L*ORD* is are my rock and my fortress and my deliverer; My God, my strength, in whom I will trust; My shield and the horn of my salvation, my stronghold. I will call upon the L*ORD*, who is worthy to be praised; So shall I be saved from my enemies. The pangs of death surrounded me, And the floods of ungodliness made me afraid. The sorrows of Sheol surrounded me; The snares of death confronted me. In my distress I called upon the L*ORD*, And cried out to my God; [You] heard my voice from [Your] temple, And my cry came before [You], even to [Your] ears.*

—PSALM 18:1–6

I stopped and looked into Yeshua's eyes, and He said from the same psalm,

I will come to you and bring My justice. Then I will shake the earth and cause it to tremble. The foundations of the hills will quake and be shaken. My righteous anger will rise up and a fiery smoke will come up from My nostrils, and such devouring fire from My mouth that coals will be kindled from it. I will bow the heavens also, and come down with the darkness under My feet and come to your aid. I will come riding upon a cherub and fly, fly upon the wings of the wind to your rescue.

I again responded, this time with understanding and faith:

The LORD thundered from heaven, And the Most High uttered His voice, Hailstones and coals of fire. He sent out arrows and scattered the foe. Lightnings in abundance, and He vanquished them. Then the channels of the sea were seen. The foundations of the world were uncovered, At Your rebuke, O LORD, At the blast of the breath of Your nostrils. [You] sent from above, [You] took me; [You] drew me out of many waters. [You] delivered me from my strong enemy, From those who hated me, For they were too strong for me. They confronted me in the day of my calamity, But the LORD was my support. [You] brought me out into a broad place; [You] delivered me because [You] delighted in me.

—PSALM 18:13–19

Then I said,

> Thank You so much for this teaching. I feel as if a great weight has been lifted off my shoulders. Now I understand and can fight a good fight and win over my thoughts and what I think in my mind. Now I know the truth that will set me free.

Yeshua held me again in His arms. He kissed me on the forehead and said,

> You are such a delight to Me. I love you so much. What a joy you are to Me!

Yeshua finished by saying,

> Thank you for spending time with Me. Your presence is such a blessing to Me. I will call you again because I need someone to share My thoughts with. I need others to spend time with and share My heart. Will you tell My other sons and daughters that I want to spend time with them too? Thank you for listening. I love you.

CHAPTER 14

ON EAGLES WINGS

❧

STOOD UPON THE mountaintop and Yeshua was standing beside me. Yeshua took hold of my hand and as I turned to look at Him, I said,

> It is always so quiet and peaceful here upon the mountain. I could stay up here and never come down."

Yeshua responded and said,

> This mountain is the place where you are to stay even when going through a storm. Do not fear the storms, but embrace them. You are to pray and ask the Father in My name regarding the storm you are in, to give you strength. He will give you His words of truth for each situation. Then mount up on the words of God's promises and songs of praise as though they were wings. Wait on the wind of the Holy Spirit; and when the wind comes by, then soar on the wind. The wind of the Spirit and the Word will carry you high above the storms, and the peace of the Father which passes all understanding will mount guard over your heart and mind."

Then Yeshua pointed to a rock high on one of the mountains. I saw an eagle standing on the edge of a cliff. His wings were extended out; and as the wind blew, the eagle flapped his wings. He flew up and caught the air current and began to soar on the wind.

As we watched this beautiful sight, Yeshua said,

> A mature eagle rarely has to flap his wings when flying. He catches the air currents and then he glides on the wind. My

Spirit is this wind. The Spirit and the Word must be in agreement and there must be a balance. When I went away I sent
the Holy Spirit to take My place. This Spirit is the Spirit of
My Father and where the Spirit is, there My Father is also.

My Father loves you so much. He doesn't want anyone
to fail, for the Father's portion is His beloved people. When
you feel you are in a desert land or when you are in a trial,
My Father will watch over you. Even as an eagle He will
circle over you and keep you in His sight and keep you
as the apple of His eye. And as an eagle stirs up her nest
and flutters over her young spreading abroad her wings and
takes her young and bears them on her wings, and so the
Father will do for those He loves if they will trust in Him.
The Father will make you ride on the high places of the
earth that you might eat the increase of the fields for the
fields are white with harvest. For the Father will bear you
on eagles wings and bring you to Himself because you obey
His voice in truth and keep His covenant, then you shall be
His own peculiar possession and treasure from among and
above all peoples for all the earth is His. The Father says
He has ordained you to be a kingdom of priests to Me, a
holy people and has consecrated you and set you apart to
worship Him. My Father will keep you from the wiles and
the snares of the devil. He has given His angels charge over
you to lift you up lest you dash your foot against a stone.
My Father says in His Word,

You whom I have taken from the ends of the earth, And
called you from its farthest regions, And said unto you,
"You are My servant. I have chosen you and have not cast
you away: Fear not, for I am with you. Do not be dis-
mayed, for I am your God. I will strengthen you, Yes, I
will help you, I will uphold you with My righteous right
hand." Behold, all that were incensed against you Shall be
ashamed and disgraced;. They shall be as nothing, And
those who strive with you shall be as nothing. You shall
seek them and not find them—Those who contended with

you. Those who war against you Shall be as nothing, As a nonexistent thing....I will make you into a new threshing sledge with sharp teeth; You shall thresh the mountains [of the enemy] and beat them small, And make the hills [hiding places of the enemy] like chaff. You shall winnow them, the wind shall carry them away, And the whirlwind shall scatter them; You shall rejoice in the Lord, And shall glory in the Holy One of [Yishrael].

—ISAIAH 41:9–12, 15–16

The Father's protection for this hour is so great, that He has you hidden in His castles and strongholds guarded by bars of iron and bronze. You are the beloved of the Lord and next to the Father you will dwell safely. The Father covers you all the day long and makes you to dwell between His shoulders. For there is none like the Father, His majestic glory illuminates the heavens, as the Father rides through the skies to your aid. The eternal Father is your refuge and dwelling place, and underneath are His everlasting arms. He drives the enemy before you and thrusts them out, saying, Destroy! For His beloved children dwell in safety, His fountain alone dwells in a land of grain and new wine. My Father will drop the dew from His heavens to water the land of His people. Rejoice, for you are blessed. For you are His beloved, saved by the Father, the shield of your help, the sword that exalts you. Your enemies will come cowering before you and submit themselves to you because of the Father's mighty power and protection. Then you shall march on the enemies' high places possessing the land in the Father's behalf.

Yeshua continued by saying,

Once you know the Father's plan to take back His land and His high places and understand the Father's great and mighty power over all the powers of darkness, then you can see that He has given you power to tread on serpents, scorpions and over all the power of the enemy. Nothing shall by

*any means hurt you. Therefore you can rise up like an eagle
and possess your blessings. You can rise up to sit in heavenly places with Me and the devil will be under your feet.
He has no power over you as long as you yield to My voice
and keep My Word in your heart.*

Again Yeshua said,

*Now is the time that the Father calls to His young eagles to
come out of the nest and soar. As a mother eagle stirs up
the down in her nest to expose the thorns and thistles, so the
Father will stir up your nest and flutter over you His young.
He will spread over you His wings and take you and bear you
on His pinions. He will take you up high on His wings and
then let you go. Even if you fall He will catch you and carry
you up high again and then drop you until you can fly and
soar on your own. The Father is always circling over you and
He keeps His eyes always upon you so that you will not fail.
As an eagle you will mount up at the Father's command and
make your nest on a high inaccessible place. On the cliff you
will dwell and remain securely upon the point of the rock, the
stronghold. From there you will spy out the prey, the enemy
and his forces. Your eyes shall see it far off and from there
you shall possess the gates of hell. You will teach your young
ones to do the same. Behold, you will come up and fly swiftly
like an eagle and spread your wings against the enemy and
his hordes. In that day the hearts of the enemy will be like
the heart of a terrified defeated foe. For you shall be swifter
than leopards and fiercer than the evening wolves. You shall
spread yourselves and press on with confidence; yes you shall
come from afar. You shall fly like an eagle that hastens to
devour the serpent. The serpent will be food for you. Your
young ones will develop a taste for the serpent to destroy him
and your young ones will be bold and not be afraid. They will
devour the prey to destroy him. The enemy is cunning for he
lays snares and traps. He pursues My chosen ones and he is
swifter than the birds of prey. He will rise up to defeat you*

and he will pursue you on the mountains and lay in wait for
you in the wilderness. It is written,

But have you not known? Have you not heard? The everlasting God, the LORD, the Creator of the ends of the earth,
Neither faints nor is weary. His understanding is unsearch-
able. He gives power to the weak, And to those who have
no might He increases strength. Even the youths shall faint
and be weary, And the young men shall utterly fall, But
those who wait on the LORD Shall renew their strength.
They shall mount up with wings like eagles, They shall run
and not be weary, They shall walk and not faint.

—ISAIAH 40:28–31

As eagles, you are to prepare the way of the Lord, make
straight and smooth a highway for the Father. Every valley
shall be lifted up, and every mountain and hill of resistance
of the enemy shall be made low. The crooked and uneven
shall be made straight and the rough places a plain. But
first, there must be a holy remnant. You have been made the
righteousness of God through Me, Messiah Yeshua Adonai.
For your worldly goodness is as filthy rags to My Father.
When you repent and turn from your worldly ways and
old ways of doing things and receive and acknowledge Me
as your Savior, you will receive Me and the righteousness
of My Father that dwells within Me. Through spending
time in His Word and allowing the Spirit of My Father
to cleanse your mind, then you will begin to submit to My
Father's will and think like He does. As an eagle you will
be fed by My Father's hand with His wisdom. The Father's
will and thoughts toward you are good and not evil for those
who belong to Him, who earnestly hunger and thirst for His
righteousness. Therefore your thoughts should be good and
not evil even towards those who do not yet believe and to
your brothers and sisters who believe.

Then Yeshua said,

The Holy Spirit's fruit or character should rule and reign in you in every situation. The love of My Father should rule over everything in your life. Then the glory of My Father shall be revealed in you, and all flesh shall see His glory together. O you, that brings good tidings, get thee up into the high mountain. O you, that brings the good news, lift up your voice with strength, lift your voice, do not be afraid. Say to the nations, Behold your God! Behold, the Lord God will come with a strong hand, and His arm shall rule for Him. Behold, His reward is with Him, and His work before Him. The Father shall feed His flock like a shepherd. He shall gather the lambs with His arm, and carry them in His bosom, and shall gently lead those that are with young. He shall be called Zaphnath-paaneah, which is, Savior of the Age.

Finally Yeshua said,

In this last battle you will be My battle ax, My weapon of war. I will give you wisdom and My plans for each battle. As we know, our battle is not with man but with principalities, powers and rulers of the air and all forms of wickedness in high places. Because you soar in heavenly places with Me, I will give you wisdom on how to respond to people when they say all manner of evil things against you or come against you. You will respond in love and not in anger. As you respond with the fruit of My Spirit, which is love, joy, peace, patience, kindness, goodness, faithfulness, meekness, and self-control, the enemy is defeated. The enemy cannot win against the fruit of My character. These weapons of our warfare are mighty through My Father for the pulling down of strongholds.

CHAPTER 15

THE EYE OF THE EAGLE

※

YESHUA SAID,

Now the Father wants to give you His wisdom and insight regarding our enemy.

Then I felt something and looked down. My arms had become wings like an eagle. I stretched out my arms, and I could see long white flowing feathers. Totally perplexed, I asked, "What are these for?"

Yeshua responded,

The Father wants to take you high above the earth so He can show you His plans for overcoming the enemy.

Then a great wind began to blow through the feathers on my wings. The great wind blew under the wings until I was lifted up. The great wind carried me high above everything. I could see the cliff where I had been, but Yeshua was not there. I looked all around for Him but could not find Him.

Fear began to take hold of me, but then Yeshua spoke in my ear,

Do not be afraid, I and the Father are one. The I Am is here. I am in the Father and the Father is in Me. When you have seen Me you have seen the Father. The Father wants to speak His wisdom and plan to you.

The Father's peace came all over me, and I found rest for my soul. When Yeshua spoke to me, I could clearly hear the Father's voice as He spoke. He said,

The eyes of the eagle represent prophetic vision that comes from the Father. The Father will reveal His heart to the prophets in these last days.

Then I heard Yeshua say, *"Look down."* When I looked down I could see the mountains all around, and as I looked closer to the earth I could see a river flowing between the mountains.

The sight in my eyes seemed to be magnified over a thousand times because I could see people walking around on the ground. I could see how they lived their lives, who was saved and who wasn't, and I could see demonic forces at work in their lives.

It was as though my eyes were opened for the first time as to what was really going on upon the earth. I could see how Satan, our enemy, was wounding, hurting, abusing, and lying to the hearts of men. Satan was lying to the hearts of men by telling them that the Father didn't love them or care about them; that the Father was the one who was causing all the hurts and pains; and that all the calamities were caused by Him. The truth is that Satan is as a roaring lion seeking whom he may devour.

I could see demonic powers overseeing nations, kingdoms, and earthly rulers. But most of all I could see the Father's holy angels in battle for the souls of men.

As I looked to the right, I could see the great host of the Father's army fighting over the kingdom of Persia.

Yeshua reminded me when He said,

The enemy's powers are strong, but the power of the Father God is mighty to the pulling down of strongholds. The god of this world lost his headship over the earth when I went to the cross. At the cross I was crucified, resurrected, and exalted to the right hand of My Father. The keys to the headship of the earth were given to Me, therefore dominion and headship were given into My hands. Now I am the God of this world; and when I come to live in you, I give you dominion. But first you must submit to My instructions and seek My face. When you seek My face, I will give you the Father's plans to pray back to Him from the earth. It's through godly prayers and praise to the Father that the

*holy angels of My Father can have victory over the powers
of darkness.*

As I soared above it all on the great wind of the Holy Spirit, there
was such a great peace and tranquility that I had not known in a
long time. I felt as though I was resting in the great and mighty
arms of my Father. I knew I was resting on the wings of my Father's
Word. For the Father's Word does not return void, it prospers in all
that it was sent to do.

Then Yeshua said,

> *As you soar up higher on the eagle's wings you will rise up
> past each new realm of the heavenlies. For in the heavenly
> realm there are demonic realms that move up according
> to order. First there is the lower realm called principali-
> ties, then there are powers, thirdly there are rulers of the
> darkness of this world, called master spirits, who are world
> rulers, and finally spirit forces of wickedness in high places.
> So when you come up higher you will rise up past these
> realms and will be able to see them at work in people and
> in nations. Our weapons are not to fight against people but
> against principalities, powers, rulers, and wickedness.*
>
> *As you rise up on eagle's wings, the Word will cover you
> with My complete armor for protection that no weapon
> of the enemy that is formed against you shall prosper. My
> armor will give you power to resist and stand your ground
> against the forces of darkness so that you will not be moved
> even when you are in a crisis. Stand therefore on the truth
> of My Word around your waist and on the integrity of My
> character as a breastplate to cover you. Cover your feet in
> preparation with the remembrance of the gospel of salva-
> tion and peace. This will cause you to stand with stability
> and not be moved by every wind of doctrine. Forever keep
> before you the knowledge of My Father's saving faith as a
> shield that will quench all the flaming missiles of the enemy.
> For you have My salvation to cover your thoughts like a
> helmet, My Word that is the very Word of My Father in
> all its power and glory, to be used against our enemy Satan.*

When you pray at all times with the help of My Spirit
which is within you, the Spirit will help you stay alert and
keep watch with strong purpose and perseverance to inter-
cede on behalf of all the saints and the nations.

As you move up higher, you will enter new realms of
faith and revelation of God's power so that you can see
more of God's glory. Remember, at all times that you sit in
heavenly places with Me and Satan is under your feet. I am
the Lord of the heavens.

Then Yeshua spoke into my ear, saying,

The Father will give you His strategy for winning the battles
over the powers of darkness in your life first and then in the
lives of others so that each one will become an overcomer.
You overcome by My blood that was poured out at the cross
and on the mercy seat and the word of your testimony. You
will not love your life unto the death. I am the Lamb that
was slain from the foundations of the world to deliver and
redeem all men from the power of sin. My Father and I
will give you the strength for the battle through the Holy
Spirit. The Father will give you His plans for defeating the
enemy in your life. The Father has spoken to your forefa-
thers in the past such as Joshua, Deborah, Gideon, David,
Peter, Paul and Silas, John, and others. These are some of
the Father's mighty, warring warriors.

As an example Yeshua explained, saying,

Deborah was a judge who ruled over a vast army and
people. The Father gave her victory by another woman
Jael whom the Father worked through to destroy the evil
demonic powers that were against them with a single tent
peg. Then Deborah sang a song of praise It is written,

Hear, O kings, give ear, O princes, I will sing to the Lord,
I will sing praise to the Lord, the God of Israel. When
You, O God, went forth out of Seir, when you marched out
of the field of Edom, the earth trembled and the heavens

dropped water. The mountains quaked at the presence of the Lord.

—JUDGES 5:3–5, AMPC

The Father used Deborah to defeat their enemy and a song of victory came forth.

Awake, awake, Deborah! Awake, awake, utter a song! Arise, Barak, and lead away your captives.

—JUDGES 5:12, AMPC

The Father used Joshua and the Father's obedient children to pull down a great stronghold. Joshua was given a plan of walking around a great city. This city was impenetrable to natural strength, but with the Father's wisdom this stronghold came down with the sound of a trumpet and a shout.

Gideon was a man full of fear because of the intimidation of the enemy. But the Father sent an Angel of the Lord to say to him,

The LORD is with you, you mighty man of valor!

—JUDGES 6:12

The Lord looked upon him and said,

Go in this might of yours and you shall save Israel from the hand of the [enemy]. Have I not sent you?

—JUDGES 6:14

In the Father's power the Spirit of the Lord came upon Gideon and his chosen. Gideon, with only three hundred men, pitchers, torches, and trumpets, totally defeated a whole nation with the Father's power and might.

Yeshua used another example and said,

In David's mighty army there were men of renown who fought with the sword for the Lord with such great power. With the power of the Father some had killed eight hundred of the demonic powers at one time. David himself was a mighty warrior for the Father. When the enemy took his

*family, David encouraged and strengthened himself in the
words of the Father. Then he inquired of the Father whether
he should overtake them. And the Father said to pursue
them and he would overtake them and recover everything
that had been taken. David and his men found the enemy
and the Father gave them a complete victory and David
recovered all. Nothing was lost and David took all the spoil
back from the enemy.*

*When David became king his enemies came up against
him two more times. It is written,*

David inquired of the Lord, saying, Shall I go up against
the Philistines? Will you deliver [them] into my hand?
And the Lord said to David, Go up for I will surely deliver
[them] into your hand. And David came to Baal-perazim,
and he smote them there, and said, The Lord has broken
through my enemies before me, like the bursting out of
great waters.

—2 SAMUEL 5:19–20, AMPC

Finally, David's enemy came against him in another place.

*When David inquired of the Lord, He said, You shall not
go up, but go behind them and come upon them over opposite the mulberry (or balsam) trees. And when you hear the
sound of marching in the tops of the mulberry trees, then
bestir yourselves, for then has the Lord gone out before you
to smite the army of the enemy.*

—2 SAMUEL 5:23–24, AMPC

*When David did as the Father asked him, the Father
destroyed all of David's enemies that had come against him.
In these final hours the battle will get fierce, and it will be
our Father's instructions that will cause us to overcome. It
may be God's plan of action to pray a prayer for deliverance to the Father God in the midst of a trial as was done
for Peter when he was thrown in prison for telling the world
about Me.*

Next Yeshua said,

> *Peter was put in prison, but prayer was made without*
> *ceasing by My people, the church, to My Father for him.*
> *Because of My Father's love and the prayer of the saints,*
> *My Father sent an angel to deliver Peter out of prison. The*
> *chains fell off and the prison doors were opened. Therefore*
> *be encouraged My Father will do the same for you when*
> *the time comes. Father's plan of deliverance came in the*
> *form of a praise song when Paul and Silas were imprisoned*
> *for preaching the kingdom of My Father and liberating a*
> *girl from Satan's grasp. After being struck with many blows,*
> *Paul and Silas were put in the deepest part of the prison*
> *where their feet were chained with stocks. It is written,*

But about midnight, as Paul and Silas were praying and
singing hymns of praise to God, and the [other] prisoners
were listening to them, Suddenly there was a great earth-
quake, so that the very foundations of the prison were
shaken; and at once all the doors were opened and everyone's shackles were unfastened. When the jailer…saw [they
were still there but free] he brought them out [of the dun-
geon] and said, Men, what is it necessary for me to do that
I might be saved. And they answered, 'Believe in the Lord
Jesus Christ [Yeshua the Messiah]…and you will be saved,
[and this applies both to] you and your household as well.
— ACTS 16:25–27, 30–31, AMPC

> *The Father delivers a great victory because of praise and*
> *prayer in the midst of tribulation. I have given you some of*
> *My Father's plans for giving you the victory. There will be*
> *others revealed in these last days.*

Again I looked down to the earth and saw the enemy forces at
work among mankind. As the Lord's body began to praise the name
of Yeshua, the Father's mighty angels went into battle and pushed
back the forces of darkness. I could see everything through the eyes
of an eagle. Then in an instant we were back on the top of the mountain. Yeshua took my hand and said,

Now that you have the eyes of an eagle there is another realm that you have seen into that I want to explain to you."

Yeshua continued on, explaining,

I have given My children eyes to see into the spirit realm. All the times you have been with Me you have seen with your spiritual eyes. Your spirit has been walking with Me. You can come into My presence each day through prayer and through praise. When you pray or praise and worship My Father, Myself, and the Holy Spirit, you enter our realm, the realm of the kingdom of heaven. You must keep your eyes on the kingdom of God and not on man or the things of the earth. The apostle John was a man who had the eyes of an eagle, for he saw the heavenly realm. In the Book of Revelation he saw the future realm and wrote about it. There were other men who also had the eyes of the eagle. In earlier times there were Moses, David, Isaiah, Jeremiah, Ezekiel, and Daniel, to name a few. I am releasing the eyes of an eagle upon those who love Me with their whole hearts. For those who love Me are My people and they will usher in and proclaim My coming. For My people are a nation of prophets, priests, and kings. John the Baptist was one of My prophets who proclaimed My coming the first time. I will need the same type of person who will see with the eyes of the eagle and will proclaim to the world what they see, even if it leads to their death. For John said,

I am the voice of one crying aloud in the wilderness.... Prepare the way of the Lord.

—JOHN 1:23, AMPC

These prophets of Mine will be all over the world to warn and proclaim that judgment is coming and the door to the ark of safety is closing up. I am that door to the ark; and he that comes to Me for safety I will in no way reject or cast away. The time is drawing short and I do not want that any should perish but that all should come to the knowledge of

Yeshua as Savior and Lord. I came to bring life and bring it abundantly.

Finally, I said,

Yeshua, thank You for showing me about having spiritual eyes, the eyes of the eagle. Now I understand that as I worship the Father, You, and the Holy Spirit, and give You all my love and adoration, You will share Your plans and secrets with me and even share Your intimate self with me. You will show me those intimate things about Yourself that only those who are closest to You, and only those who get close enough to You to lean their heads on Your breast, can know. We can experience the fullness of who You are. You are the Lion and the Lamb. For You are the Lion to those who are stubborn and rebellious, to those who will not listen to the call of the Lamb. You are the Lamb to all who will listen and obey the call of the Lamb.

Again, Yeshua spoke,

I cry out to those who will humble themselves to hear My voice. It is written,

Come to Me, all you who labor and are heavy laden, and I will give you rest. Take My yoke upon you and learn of Me, for I am gentle and lowly in heart, and you will find rest for your souls. For My yoke is easy and My burden is light.
—MATTHEW 11:28–30

Yeshua turned and looked into my eyes and said,

There are so many who don't know about My Father's love.

When Yeshua said this, I could see tears welling up in His eyes. My heart was so moved by His compassion and love that I reached my hand out and I touched His cheek. There was such tenderness in His eyes that I began to weep with Him.

Then He said to me,

Help Me to tell others that the time is short. The Father desires that none should perish, but that all come to repentance and the knowledge of the Lord.

I responded by saying, "I will do my best to help you."
Finally Yeshua said,

Thank you for pressing in and being an overcomer with Me. I will keep you and hold you up during these last day trials and persecutions.

Yeshua pulled me into His arms and held me close to His chest. I rested in His loving arms and was refreshed. I just stayed there in His arms and didn't move until He released me and said,

It's time for you to go back to encourage and tell others I am coming soon.

With one last look into my eyes, He said,

I love you!

CHAPTER 16

HEAVENLY WARRIOR

❧

THERE WAS A great shout and I stood in the midst of thousands of others as we joined together in front of our beloved warrior King, the Savior of the world.

Then I saw Him as He is in all His glory. As the Word says, He was

> [One] like the Son of Man; clothed with a robe which reached to His feet and with a girdle of gold about His breast. His head and hair were like white wool, [as white] as snow, and His eyes [flashed] like a flame of fire. His feet glowed like burnished (bright) bronze as it is refined in a furnace, and His voice was like the sound of many waters. In His right hand He held seven stars, and from His mouth there came forth a sharp two-edged sword, and His face was like the sun shining in full power at midday.
> —REVELATION 1:13–16, AMPC

In His presence we were all so overwhelmed that we fell to our knees, some fell face down, and we worshipped Him as the King of kings and the Lord of lords.

We had come before Him to get our instructions and directions in this our final battle. Then Yeshua began to speak. As we all got to our feet, He spoke from His Word,

> Be careful that no one misleads you.... For many will come in...My name..., saying, I am the Christ (the Messiah); and they will lead many astray. And you will hear of wars and rumors of wars; see that you are not frightened or troubled, for this must take place, but the end is not yet. For nation will rise against nation and kingdom against

kingdom, and there will be famines and earthquakes in place after place; All this is but the beginning [the early pains] of the birth pangs [of the intolerable anguish]. Then they will hand you over to suffer affliction and tribulation and put you to death, and you will be hated by all nations for My name's sake. And then many will be offended and repelled and will begin to distrust and desert [Him whom they ought to trust and obey] and will stumble and fall away and betray one another and pursue one another with hatred. And many false prophets will rise up and deceive and lead many into error. And the love of the great body of people will grow cold because of the multiplied lawlessness and iniquity. But he who endures to the end will be saved. And this good news of the kingdom (the Gospel) will be preached throughout the whole world as a testimony to all the nations, and then will come the end....

For just as the lightning flashes from the east and shines and is seen as far as the west, so will the coming of the Son of man be....

Immediately after the tribulation of those days the sun will be darkened, and the moon will not shed its light, and the stars will fall from the sky, and the powers of the heavens will be shaken. Then the sign of the Son of man will appear in the sky, and then all the tribes of the earth will mourn and beat their breasts and lament in anguish, and they will see the Son of man coming on the clouds of heaven with power and great glory.... And He will send out His angels with a loud trumpet call, and they will gather His elect from the four winds, [even] from one end of the universe to the other....

If anyone says to you then, Behold, here is the Christ (the Messiah)! Or, There He is!—do not believe it. For false [Messiah's] and false prophets will arise, and they will show great signs and wonders, so as to deceive and lead astray, if possible, even the elect....

At that time two men will be in the field; one will be taken and one will be left. Two women will be grinding at the hand mill; one will be taken and one will be left. Watch therefore..., for you do not know in what kind of a day...your Lord is coming....

You also must be ready therefore; for the Son of man is coming at an hour when you do not expect Him. Who then is the faithful, thoughtful, and wise servant, whom his master has put in charge of his household to give to the others the food and supplies at the proper time? Blessed...is that servant whom, when his master comes, he will find so doing. I solemnly declare to you, he will set him over all his possessions. But if that servant is wicked and says to himself, My master is delayed and is going to be gone a long time, And begins to beat his fellow servants and to eat and drink with the drunken, The master of that servant will come on a day when he does not expect him and at an hour of which he is not aware. And I will punish him...and put him with the pretenders (hypocrites); there will be weeping and grinding of teeth.

—MATTHEW 24:4–14, 27, 29–31,
23–24, 40–42, 44–51, AMPC

Then Yeshua said,

We must be watchful and be about the Father's business so that none would be deceived or left behind. I have called you here as My mighty warriors for I am the warrior King who gives you the strategy for battle. We are entering this battle so that My Father's kingdom will come on earth as it is in heaven. The battle we are fighting is not against flesh and blood but against principalities, powers, rulers of the air and against spiritual wickedness in heavenly places. The enemy has released some of his most powerful weapons against us. But I am your light and your salvation, whom shall you fear or dread? I am the refuge and stronghold of your life; of whom shall you be afraid? When the wicked, even your enemies and your foes, come upon you to eat up your flesh, they will stumble and fall. Though a host encamp against you, your heart shall not fear. Though war arise against you, be confident for I have overcome.

If you will seek My face and require My presence as your vital need then in the day of trouble, I will hide you in My shelter; in the secret place of My tent I will hide you; I will set you high upon a rock. I will teach you My ways and lead you in a plain and even path. Be strong in Me; be empowered through your union with Me. You will receive My strength; which My boundless might provides.

Put on all the armor that I provide for you that you may be able successfully to stand up against all the strategies and the deceits of the devil. Therefore, put on the Father's complete armor, that you may be able to resist and stand your ground on the evil day of danger and having done all the crisis demands, to stand firmly in your place, stand therefore and hold your ground by standing fast on all the promises that My Father has given you of all His delivering power. Pray at all times, on every occasion, in every season by the Spirit's power with all manner of prayer and entreaty.

You must keep alert and watch with strong purpose and perseverance, interceding in behalf of all the saints. For I have given you power to tread on serpents and scorpions and over all the power of the enemy and nothing shall by any means hurt you. I have made you strong through Me, and the power of My might. All power and authority has been given into My hands by My Father, therefore seek My face daily for the wisdom about the battle. Again I remind you to daily stand and hold your ground having tightened the belt of truth around your loins, speaking My truth in love always, and having put on the breastplate of My integrity and of moral rectitude and right standing with God, which protects your heart. Finally, in preparation to face the enemy I want you to shod your feet with firm-footed stability, promptness, and readiness. These are produced by the good news of the gospel of peace. Over everything, lift up the covering shield of saving faith. This is that with which

*you can quench all the flaming missiles of the wicked one.
Put on the helmet of salvation and take up the sword of the
Spirit, which is the Word of God.*

Again Yeshua said,

*Now I remind you to be watchful for your enemy comes as
a roaring lion seeking whom he may devour. Regarding my
kingdom, as it is written,*

It is like a man who was about to take a long journey, and
he called his servants together and entrusted them with his
property. To one he gave five talents..., to another two, to
another one—to each in proportion to his own personal
ability. Then he departed and left the country. He who
had received the five talents went at once and traded them,
and he gained five talents more. And likewise he who had
received the two talents—he also gained two talents more.
But he who had received the one talent went and dug a hole
in the ground and hid his master's money.

Now after a long time the master of those servants
returned and settled accounts with them. And he who had
received the five talents came and brought him five more,
saying, Master, you entrusted to me five talents; see, here
I have gained five talents more. His master said to him,
Well done, you upright...and faithful servant! You have
been faithful and trustworthy over a little; I will put you
in charge of much. Enter into and share the joy (the delight
and blessedness) which your master enjoys.

And he also who had the two talents came forward,
saying, Master, you entrusted two talents to me; here
I have gained two talents more. His master said to him,
Well done, you upright and faithful servant! You have
been faithful and trustworthy over a little; I will put you
in charge of much. Enter and share the joy...which your
master enjoys.

He who had received the one talent also came forward,
saying, Master, I knew you to be a harsh and hard man,

reaping where you did not sow, and gathering where you had not winnowed......So I was afraid and I went and hid your talent in the ground. Here you have what is your own. But his master answered him, You wicked and lazy and idle servant! Did you indeed know that I reap where I have not sowed and gather...where I have not winnowed? Then you should have invested my money with the bankers, and at my coming I would have received what was my own with interest. So take the talent away from him and give it to the one who has the ten talents.

For to everyone who has will more be given, and he will be furnished richly so that he will have abundance...And throw the good-for-nothing servant into the outer darkness; there will be weeping and grinding of teeth. When the Son of man comes in His glory (His majesty and splendor), and all the holy angels with Him, then He will sit on the throne of His glory....Watch therefore...for you know neither the day nor the hour when the Son of man will come.

—MATTHEW 25:14–31, 13, AMPC

Yeshua continued speaking from His Word:

From the fig tree learn its lesson; as soon as its young shoots become soft and tender and it puts out its leaves, you know of a surety that summer is near. So also when you see these signs, all taken together, coming to pass, you may know of a surety that [I am] near, at the very doors. Truly I tell you, this generation (the whole multitude of people living at that same time...) will not pass away till all these things taken together take place. Sky and earth will pass away, but My words will not pass away. But of that [exact] day and hour no one knows, not even the angels of heaven, nor the Son, but only the Father.

—MATTHEW 24:32–36, AMPC

Then Yeshua said,

Again I say be watchful and draw close to Me, keep your eyes on Me for I am the only one who knows the strategy and the way, because I keep My eyes on the Father. For I am the way, the truth and the life for no one comes to the Father but by Me. As you keep your eyes on Me, I will give you new strategies in prayer. True heavenly warriors are those watchmen on the walls praying and interceding with the Holy Spirit leading and giving you wisdom regarding the enemy's strategies. I will open your spiritual eyes to see in the heavenly realm just like I did for Elisha's servant. In My Word it says,

[Elisha] answered, Fear not; for those with us are more than those with them. Then Elisha prayed, Lord, I pray You open his eyes that he may see. And the Lord opened the young man's eyes, and he saw, and behold, the mountain was full of horses and chariots of fire roundabout Elisha.

—2 KINGS 6:16–17, AMPC

My Word also says,

Pray at all times (on every occasion, in every season) in the Spirit, with all manner of prayer and entreaty. To that end keep alert and watch with strong purpose and perseverance, interceding on behalf of all the saints.

—EPHESIANS 6:18, AMPC

Then He looked at me and said,

We will be together soon, so trust in Me and stay abiding in Me and stay close.

CHAPTER 17

THE FINAL BATTLE

❧

THE FINAL BATTLE for the souls of men had begun with all the forces of darkness. Our Beloved, the Savior of the world, was in our midst as we fought for the last revival before Yeshua comes to take His bride to the wedding feast.

The forces of darkness came in like a dark cloud. We had on all of God's armor, for the weapons of our warfare are not carnal but mighty through our Father to the pulling down of strongholds, casting down arguments, theories, and reasonings and every proud and lofty thing that sets itself up against the true knowledge of the Father; and leading every thought and purpose away captive into the obedience of Yeshua, the Messiah, the Anointed One. We were in readiness to punish every insubordinate for his disobedience until we were fully secured and complete. Then no weapon that was formed against us could prosper.

The Lord began speaking by saying,

I have come to awaken the sleepers!

Then He began speaking to all the warriors gathered and saying from His Word,

Take no part in and have no fellowship with the fruitless deeds and enterprises of darkness, but instead [let your lives be so in contrast as to] expose and reprove and convict them. For it is a shame even to speak of or mention the things that [such people] practice in secret. But when anything is exposed and reproved by the light, it is made visible and clear; and where everything is visible and clear there is light. Therefore He says, Awake, O sleeper, and arise from the dead in spirit, and Christ shall shine…upon you and give you light.

—EPHESIANS 5:11–14, AMPC

Yeshua continued by saying,

Accordingly then, let us not sleep. Let us not be drawn by the world into drowsiness and slumber, but keep wide awake, alert, watchful, cautious, and on our guard and let us be sober. Rouse yourselves and keep awake and alert; strengthen and invigorate what remains and so call to your remembrance the lessons that I have already taught you. Continually lay them to heart and obey them and repent. Prepare your hearts and repent. If you do not rouse your-selves and keep awake and watch, I will come upon you like a thief, and you will not know or suspect at what hour I will come. Behold, I am coming as a thief! Blessed is he who stays awake and alert and who guards his clothes, so that he may not be naked and seen exposed.

Be full of the oil of the Holy Spirit at all times and be like the five virgins who had plenty of oil in their lamps, for when I come suddenly they will be ready to come in with Me.

Yeshua continued by saying,

Awaken the watchmen! I have set you watchmen upon your walls who will never hold their peace day or night; you will put My Lord in remembrance in prayer of My promises, keep not silence, and give the Lord God no rest until His plans are established. The watchmen will stand as priests before the Lord with crying out and tears for the souls of men. This last great harvest of the souls of the men, women, and children must come in. I have extended mercy and grace but the door of mercy and grace is going to shut and My wrath will be poured out upon the earth. For those left behind there will be great tribulation. Unless the people repent and turn to Me, I will not be able to stop the destroyer. Just like it was for the Egyptians of old, all the

*plagues and calamities will come upon the whole earth. But
I will still have witnesses at that time on the earth. During
the tribulation period I will unleash all My wrath upon the
earth, for My Spirit was with them, but they still did not
repent. At this time My Spirit will be taken away from the
earth."*

Yeshua then said,

*And I will prepare destroyers against thee, everyone with
his weapons; and they shall cut down thy choice cedars and
cast them into the fire. And many nations shall pass by this
city, and they shall say every man to his neighbor, where-
fore hath the Lord done thus unto this great city? Then they
shall answer, because they have forsaken the covenant of the
Lord their God, and worshiped other gods and served them.
But because thou hast kept the word of My patient endurance and have held fast the lesson of My patience with the
expectant endurance that I give you, I also will keep you
safe from the hour of trial and testing which is coming on
the whole world to try those who dwell upon the earth.*

Then the Lord opened my eyes and I could see the earth as He
saw it, and I was appalled at what He saw. I looked and saw every
man in the chambers of his imagery. For they say, the Lord sees us
not; the Lord has forsaken the earth. Even in the houses of the Lord
were people with their backs toward the temple of the Lord, and
their faces toward the east; as they worshipped the sun toward the
east, I wept.

And the Lord said from His Word,

*Cause them that have charge over the city to draw near,
even every man with his destroying weapon in his hand.
And, behold, six men came from the way of the higher gate,
which lieth toward the north, and every man a slaughter
weapon in his hand; and one man among them was clothed
with linen, with a writer's inkhorn by his side: and they
went in, and stood beside the brazen altar. And the glory of
the God of Israel was gone up from the cherub, whereupon*

he was, to the threshold of the house. And he called to the man clothed with linen which, had the writer's inkhorn by his side; and the LORD said unto him, Go through the midst of the city, and through the midst of [the earth] and set a mark upon the foreheads of the men [and women and children] that sigh and that cry for all the abominations that be done in the midst thereof. [For the enemy Satan has no power to take their souls.]

And to the others He said in my hearing, Go ye after him through the city and the earth and smite: let not your eye spare, neither have ye pity. Slay utterly old and young, both maids, and little children, and women [and men]: but do not come near any man [or woman or child] upon whom is the mark.... The iniquity of [the earth] is exceeding great, and the land is full of blood, and the city full of perverseness, for they say, the LORD has forsaken the earth and the LORD seeth not. And as for me also, mine eye shall not spare, neither will I have pity, but I will recompense their way upon their head. And behold, the man clothed with linen, which had the inkhorn by his side, reported the matter, saying, I have done as thou hast commanded me.

—EZEKIEL 9:1–6, 9–11, KJV

Yeshua said unto me,

Our enemy Satan was thrown down to earth and given power, and the Father's protective hand has been taken away from those of the earth. Satan was given power to seduce and deceive mankind. Therefore be glad, O heavens and you that dwell in them! But woe to you, O earth and sea, for the devil has come down to you in fierce anger, because he knows that he has only a short time left.

So, Satan, the dragon was furious at the woman, and he went away to wage war on the remainder of her descendants, who obey the Father's commandments and who have the testimony of Messiah Yeshua. Then I saw that there was much persecution, pain, and

torture by the enemy of the Lord's beloved bride; but she overcame
him by means of the blood of her Savior, the Lamb, and by the word
of her testimony for she did not love her life even when faced with
death for the Lord was with her.

But even in the midst of trials and persecution, those that belong
to Yeshua knew that Yeshua would not leave them nor forsake them
nor would He leave them comfortless. They knew that they were
being prepared, being set apart, and being purified by fire to rule
and reign by the side of their Yeshua forever.

My Beloved and I stood side by side in the heavenlies and fought
a good fight. I was dressed in His armor of light, and He gave me
great wisdom and strategy to fight for His people. For my beloved
Yeshua my Savior has given me the victory! For Yeshua my Savior
has made me more than a conqueror. I know that I will be victorious in all things.

CHAPTER 18

THE BRIDE

✥

SOON AFTER, THE final time came that my beloved Yeshua my Savior called to me. This time I found myself in His chariot of fire. He had sent His angel for me, and His angel said to me, "The Lord beckons you, and you are to prepare for Him and to come into His palace today." The coach we traveled in was lined with deep red burgundy velvet. The color reminded me of the blood that He shed for me that restored my relationship back to the Father. The angel delivered me to the place of preparation, to make ready for the palace visit. I had my lamp lit with plenty of extra oil; ready for Him.

We arrived at the place of preparation, not very far away from the palace. Many women there came out to meet us, and they were all set to begin to get me ready. To start, I was set in warm bath water, and as I sat there I felt wonderful cleansing all over. The water was scented with cinnamon, aloes, myrrh, and filled with glycerin. The fragrances reminded me of my Lord and how He had been anointed with such spices. The women spoke of this as purification and cleansing from the evil of the world, and this was in preparation to see my Beloved.

After the bath, oil of myrrh scented with spices of cinnamon and vanilla was rubbed all over my body. I had just been sanctified and set apart for my Beloved. I was so excited as I thought on how close I was to being with Him eternally! I considered all the times I had been in His presence, had gazed upon Him, had conversed openly with Him, and had walked together with Him in the garden. Yet it seemed almost an eternity having been only betrothed to Him, and finally our wedding was coming. I would finally be His bride in marriage, and I will be His queen, abiding and reigning with Him throughout eternity.

The women then brought in the wedding garments. First came the undergarments of silk and lace. Next came the long slip, with a hem made of a blood red ribbon sewn all around the border. I could tell it was a gift from my Beloved, for it was another reminder of His sacrifice for me. At last, they brought in the wedding dress, pure white without spot or wrinkle, just as He promised me. The sleeves were long, and the skirt went all the way to the floor. It was made of fine white linen inwrought with gold and silver. They had placed a band around my head and hanging on either side of my face were ornamental cut pieces of gold and silver with little gemstones. Around my neck was the same gold and silver with gemstones.

I looked at myself in the mirror, and I saw Him standing there beside me. I was so taken by His presence that I almost lost my breath in the excitement and anticipation of all that was coming. My hair was adorned with the rose of Sharon and the lily of the valley. My face blushed for the excitement of my Beloved coming to see me. The women flurried all around me with the final touches before I was to be presented in the palace as bride to my Master and my Beloved, the Bridegroom.

Through all the preparation, I was able to find out details on how and when my Beloved would come for me. The secret was out. My Beloved would come as a thief in the night and steal me away and take me to His palace. That night I rejoiced in joyful anticipation, and I began to praise my God that He had kept me for such a time as this. Suddenly, there was a sound at the door. I checked myself over, and I was confident that after much preparation I was ready for Him.

I opened the door and Yeshua was standing there, all clothed in His wedding garments. He said,

> This is the day I have so long waited for, and finally it has come. Come, My bride, let us go to the wedding. The banquet has been prepared, the guests have all arrived, and Father awaits.

Out of a heart overflowing with love, I spoke these love words:

My beloved Yeshua is mine and I am His. He takes me to His banqueting table; His banner over me is love. I will praise Him with my mouth, my praises are a sweet sacrifice to His ears. His name is to be exalted above every name, Messiah Yeshua Adonai, for He is my Lord and Master. I have yielded my whole heart and soul to Him, for He is truly King. I have given Him total control over every part of my being. What a delight to totally yield myself over to His love.

Then my beloved Yeshua my Savior said,

I too have waited, and all creation has awaited this moment.

CHAPTER 19

THE MARRIAGE SUPPER

❧

Then, as we rode away into the night, Yeshua began speaking to me of the effort that had been taken to invite all the wedding guests. He said,

Father has arranged and prepared this marriage for us. He has sent forth His servants to call His guests to the wedding, but they rejected His servants and would not come. He told His servants to go back and tell those guests that the wedding dinner is prepared with the fatted oxen and cattle, and all is ready; bid them to come. But the guests made light of the matter and continued on their way, one to his farm another to his business. Another made an excuse saying that a piece of real estate was just purchased and it was necessary to see the property, so he asked to be excused. Another said he purchased livestock, five yoke of oxen, and had to go test them. Another said he just got married and could not make it. The rest of the invited guests simply treated His servants harshly, and some of them were even killed for having tried to invite those guests.

When Father heard of this He was really angry. He sent out His warriors and had them execute those murderers, destroy their cities, and burn them to the ground. Father said to His servants that the wedding guests who were invited and didn't show were unworthy to be called His guests. And He told them to go into the highways, and as many as were seen there, to invite them all to come to the marriage. The servants went out and came to the highways, and gathered together all as many as they found, both bad

and good. So, our wedding has been furnished with guests.
When Father came to see the guests, He saw a man not
wearing a wedding garment or the kind of clothing that had
been tried by fire. And so Father asked him how he got in
without a wedding garment. The man was speechless. Then
Father told His servants to bind that man hand and foot,
take him out of there, and to cast him into outer darkness
where there is weeping and the gnashing of teeth. Father
did this because there are many who were called, but only
a few were chosen.

We arrived at the palace, and we sat at the grand banquet table
in the presence of all our friends and family. Everyone had come
to celebrate this union. We had truly become one; no longer two,
but one. It was wonderful to know that He was truly mine and
I was truly His. We belonged to each other. When I looked into
His eyes, I saw His love for me had not diminished at all, but had
increased. I became filled as I just drank in, like new wine, all the
love He poured out to me right from His eyes. I was so filled I just
lost myself in Him. I couldn't wait until we left so that we could be
alone together at last.

Everyone sat around the table and Yeshua took a cup of wine and
said,

I told you that I would not drink again of this fruit of the
vine until that day when I drink it new with you in My
Father's kingdom. Today is that day.

Yeshua then took bread and blessed it, He broke the bread and it
multiplied so everyone got a piece. Then He said, as He had done
with the disciples,

Take, eat; this is My body.

—MATTHEW 26:26

Everyone then received a cup of wine. Yeshua took His cup, gave
thanks, and said,

Drink from it, all of you. For this is My blood of the new
covenant, which is shed for many for the remission of sins.
—MATTHEW 26:27–28

Then He said,

Welcome to My Father's kingdom!

The banquet food that had been prepared was so incredibly deli-
cious with broiled meat, roasted pheasant, and steamed vegetables.
But that which truly satisfies are His words of love when He speaks
to me. My hunger and thirst are only satisfied as He utters His love
words to me. He leaned close to me and placed His arm around my
waist and whispered,

*I can't wait until you and I are finally alone together. Then
you will truly know the full expression of My love for you!*

He gazed into my eyes, and again I became lost in His presence.
All the thoughts of everything I loved about Him danced through
my mind,

*My Beloved is so wonderful and beautiful to me. His arms
are so strong that He can bend a bow of bronze. He is full
of the wisdom of His Father. He calls all the creatures by
name, and He is able to calm the raging seas with the wave
of His hand, and the vast oceans humbly submit to His
command. My Beloved is altogether lovely. Again I will
bless His mighty name, and my praise for Him shall continually proceed forth from my mouth.*

I said to Him.

*Now I can call You "Ishi," husband, for You are irrevocably
mine, and I, my Beloved, am Yours. For there is neither
height, nor depth, nor principalities, nor powers of darkness, nor things above, nor things below, nor things present,
nor things to come, that can ever quench the love we have
for each other.*

CHAPTER 20

THE WEDDING

❧

THEN FROM BEHIND us, we heard the sound of many trumpets signaling an announcement. We heard the voice of a great multitude, as it were, the sound of mighty rushing water. In unison they proclaimed,

Alleluia! Alleluia! Alleluia! The Lord God omnipotent reigns! Let us be glad and rejoice and give Him honor! For the marriage of Yeshua has come, and His bride has been made ready! And she has been dressed in clean, white fine linen: fine linen is the righteousness of the saints! Blessed are those who are called to the marriage supper of the Lamb!

I heard an angel say, "Your procession has come into view. O God, the procession of my God and King into the sanctuary. In front are the singers, after them the musicians, with them are the maidens playing tambourines."

Then I heard the voice of the heavenly Father ring out as He spoke to Yeshua,

You are fairer than the children of men; graciousness is poured upon Your lips; therefore [I] have blessed You forever.... Your throne, O God, is forever and ever; the scepter of righteousness is the scepter of Your kingdom. You love righteousness, uprightness, and right standing with [Me] and hate wickedness; therefore [I], Your God, [have] anointed You with the oil of gladness above your fellows. Your garments are all fragrant with myrrh, aloes, and cassia; stringed instruments make You glad. King's daughters are among Your honorable women; at Your right hand

stands the queen in gold of Ophir.... The king's daughter
in the inner part [of the palace] is all glorious; her clothing
is inwrought with gold. She [has been] brought to the king
in raiment of needlework; with the virgins, her compan-
ions that follow her, she has been brought to You. With
gladness and rejoicing they [have been] brought; where
they will enter into the King's palace.... I [have made] Your
name to be remembered in all generations; therefore, shall
the people praise and give you thanks forever and ever.
                              —PSALM 45:2, 6–9, 13–15, 17, AMPC

The trumpets sounded again, signaling to let the festivities com-
mence. Everyone began singing and rejoicing. There were dancers
everywhere with tambourines. Glory was on everyone's face.
Everyone was singing and clapping and rejoicing because what they
had long awaited had finally come.

In the midst of all the rejoicing, as we stood there, Yeshua and
I turned slowly around overlooking the great and bountiful harvest.
And then we faced each other, and looked each other over. All became
completely silent, as everyone instantly stopped in anticipation to hear
the covenant vows Yeshua and I were about to recite. Then in a voice
for all to hear, Yeshua looked intently into my eyes and began to speak
these wonderful words from His Word:

Behold thou art fair; thou hast doves' eyes. Behold thou art
fair, my beloved, yea, pleasant:...How fair is thy love, my
sister, my spouse! how much better is thy love than wine!
and the smell of thine ointments than all spices! Thy lips,
O my spouse, drop as the honeycomb: honey and milk are
under thy tongue; and the smell of thy garments is like
the smell of Lebanon. A garden enclosed is my sister, my
spouse; a spring shut up, a fountain sealed. Thy plants are
an orchard with pleasant fruits;...A fountain of gardens, a
well of living waters, and streams from Lebanon....Thou
art all fair, my love; there is no spot in thee. Come with
me from Lebanon, my spouse, with me from Lebanon;
look from the top of Amana, from the top of Shenir and
Hermon, from the lion's dens, from the mountains of

the leopards. Thou hast ravished my heart, my sister, my spouse; thou hast ravished my heart with one of thine eyes....How fair is they love, my sister, my spouse! how much better is thy love than wine!

—Song of Solomon 1:15–16; 4:10–13, 15, 7–10, kjv

I also opened my heart to Him, and began to recite to Him my covenant vows:

You, O Lord, are the King of kings and the Lord of lords. You rule and reign over the heavens and the earth and all the nations shall bow down and worship You, My beloved Yeshua, my Savior and the Savior of the world.

Then I continued reciting from His Word,

My beloved is white and ruddy, the chiefest among ten thousand. [Your] head is as the most fine gold, [Your] locks are bushy, and black as a raven. Your eyes are as the eyes of doves by the rivers of waters, washed with milk, and fitly set. [Your] cheeks are as a bed of spices, as sweet flowers; [Your] lips like lilies, dropping sweet smelling myrrh. [Your] hands are as gold rings set with the beryl: [Your belly] is as bright ivory overlaid with sapphires. [Your] legs are as pillars of marble, set upon sockets of fine gold: [Your] countenance is as Lebanon, excellent as the cedars. [Your] mouth is most sweet: yea, [You] are altogether lovely.

—Song of Solomon 5:10–16, kjv

Then I turned to everyone and said,

This is my beloved Yeshua my Savior, and this is my friend!

Chapter 21

THE BRIDAL CHAMBER

YESHUA BROUGHT ME into the wedding chamber and said,

My banner over you is love.

He put His arms around me and held me tight. I began to weep because what I had waited for so long had finally come. The air was filled with the soft sounds of flutes playing "Amazing Grace." The sounds permeated the room like a soft breeze flowing and gently touching my skin.

Yeshua held me in His arms and then He took my face in His hands and kissed me gently on the left cheek, then the right cheek, on the forehead and then at last He kissed me on the lips. I put my arms around His neck and held Him tight as He kissed me again. Yeshua poured out all of His love for me. His love encircled me, swirled and surrounded me until I was totally consumed with His passion and His love.

Yeshua then spoke and said,

> *I have brought you higher and higher into Myself. Now we are no longer two, but one, for now you have totally lost yourself in Me. My Father says the two shall become one flesh.*

Yeshua again spoke,

> *Again I say, we are no longer two but we have now become one because you have lost yourself in Me.*

I responded by saying, "How can that be?"
Yeshua answered and said,

*Because you have made the decision to surrender yourself
and your will so that you no longer control your life but
have yielded yourself into Me.*

Again Yeshua held me in His arms, and this time I melted into His love. Every door of my heart was open and every room was filled with His love. His words, "I love you," echoed through every part of my being over and over, whispering and then shouting, "I love you! I love you! I love you!" His love was filling all the empty waste places. Now I am whole again because He loves me.

I was no longer me, but I became Him in all His fullness. At last I saw things from His eyes. I was able to love the unlovable, the sinners, the wicked, the murderers, and even those who persecuted and physically abused me. Out of the deep well of the love of Yeshua where I was now abiding; His love was an endless river flowing and flowing and flowing. That which I had waited for so long had finally come. I was now flowing with that river of love. I was flowing in Him, through Him, and with Him. For He was that river of love flowing, flowing, flowing, and touching, touching, touching everyone. Wherever the river flowed people were healed, delivered, and set free; and I was one with the river. This river was as God's Word says,

> The river of the water of life, as clear as crystal, flowing from the throne of God and of the Lamb down the middle of the great street of the city. On each side of the river stood the tree of life, bearing twelve crops of fruit, yielding its fruit every month. And the leaves of the trees are for the healing of the nations. No longer will there be any curse. The throne of God and of the Lamb will be in the city and his servants will serve Him. They will see his face, and his name will be on their foreheads. There will be no more night. They will not need the light of a lamp or the light of the sun, for the Lord God will give them light. And they will reign for ever and ever.
>
> —REVELATION 22:1–5, NIV

Then Yeshua began to sing a song to me from His Word,

Sing, O Daughter of Zion; shout, O Israel! Rejoice, be in
high spirits and glory with all your heart, O daughter of
Jerusalem [in that day]. [For then it will be that] the Lord
has taken away the judgments against you; He has cast out
your enemy. The King of Israel, even the Lord [Himself],
is in the midst of you; [and after He has come to you] you
shall not experience or fear evil any more. In that day it shall
be said to Jerusalem, Fear not, O Zion. Let not your hands
sink down or be slow and listless. The Lord your God is in
the midst of you, a Mighty One, a Savior, [Who saves]! He
will rejoice over you with joy; He will rest [in silent satisfac-
tion] and in His love He will be silent and make no mention [of past sins, or even recall them]; He will exult over
you with singing. I will gather those belonging to you...who
yearn and grieve for the solemn assembly [and the festivals],
on whom...the reproach of it is a burden. Behold, at that
time I will deal with all those who afflict you; I will save the
limping [ones] and gather the outcasts and will make them a
praise and a name in every land of their shame. At that time
I will bring you in; yes, at that time I will gather you, for I
will make you a name and a praise among all the nations of
the earth when I reverse your captivity before your eyes.

—ZEPHANIAH 3:14–20, AMPC

Yeshua continued with more of His Word,

And I will make the lame a remnant, and those who were
cast off a strong nation; and [I] shall reign over them in
Mount Zion from this time forth and forever. And you, O
tower of the flock, the hill and stronghold of the Daughter
of Zion, unto you the former dominion shall come, the
kingdom of the Daughter of Jerusalem.

—MICAH 4:7–8, AMPC

Chapter 22

HIS KINGDOM COME

❧

BEFORE I KNEW it we were standing before His throne. Yeshua stood there in all His glory. Again we saw Him in His magnificence. He was clothed in fine white linen with a band of pure gold about His chest and a crown of pure gold upon His head which looked like a crown of thorns. This was a continual reminder of what He had done for all. His body was a golden luster like beryl, His face had the appearance of lightning, His eyes like flaming torches, His arms and His feet like glowing burnished bronze and the sound of His voice was like the noise of a multitude or the roaring of the sea.

We all bowed and worshipped Him. His presence was so overwhelming that I could not stand. He came over to me and touched me and that radiance came upon me and I was changed into the fullness of His glory. Then He put a crown of pure gold upon my head, and when He did I was so overcome that I fell to the ground weeping. I was so overwhelmed with gratitude that all I could do was weep. When I had recovered I took the crown that was upon my head and placed it in His hands and said,

> *All honor and power unto You, Yeshua, King of kings and Lord of lords! And unto You, Lord Yeshua, every knee does bow of every tribe and nation, every kindred and every tongue. Unto You, Lord Yeshua, every tongue does confess, that You, Yeshua, are Messiah, the Anointed Son of God and Lord of All! Your kingdom has truly come!*

Everyone began to join in the adoration and praise of the Lord. And the people cried, "Holy, holy, holy!"

For unto us a Child is born, Unto us a Son is given; And the government will be upon His shoulder. And His name will be called Wonderful, Counselor, Mighty God, Everlasting Father, Prince of Peace. Of the increase of His government and peace There will be no end, Upon the throne of David and over His kingdom, To order it and to establish it with judgment and with justice from that time forward, even forever. The zeal of the LORD of hosts will perform this.

—ISAIAH 9:6–7

The four living creatures proclaimed over and over,

Holy, holy, holy is the Lord God Almighty, Who was and is and is to come.

—REVELATION 4:8

Seraphim cried out, saying,

Holy, holy, holy is the LORD of hosts; The whole earth is full of His glory!

—ISAIAH 6:3

And then a great and mighty voice issued from the throne, saying,

This is My beloved Son, in whom I am well pleased. Yeshua must take His rightful place on the throne as sovereign Ruler of all creation.

We were then escorted by angels on one side and saints on the other to the throne of His glory. Up above the throne was what appeared to be a banner with the glorious words upon it: KING OF KINGS AND LORD OF LORDS. Beneath were the words, "HE SHALL REIGN FOREVER."

There was a rainbow near and around the throne. It gave off a glow that was the color of emerald. Also near and around the throne were twenty-four seats and upon the seats were twenty-four elders sitting, clothed in white raiment; and they had on their heads crowns of gold. And the twenty-four elders began to fall down before Yeshua and worshipped Him who lives for ever and ever, and cast their crowns before the throne, saying,

> You are worthy, O Lord, To receive glory and honor and power; For You created all things, And by Your will they exist and were created
>
> —Revelation 4:11

And the elders began to sing a new song, saying,

> Thou art worthy to take the book, and to open the seals thereof: for thou wast slain, and hast redeemed us to God by thy blood out of every kindred, and tongue, and people, and nation; and hast made us unto our God kings and priests: and we shall reign on the earth.
>
> —Revelation 5:9–10, kjv

And I beheld, and I heard the voice of many angels, and the elders, and all the saints near and around the throne, and the number of the multitude gathered were thousands upon thousands of angels, and an innumerable number of saints. Altogether we began saying over and over with a loud voice,

> Worthy is the Lamb that was slain to receive power, and riches, and wisdom, and strength, and honor, and glory, and blessing.
>
> —Revelation 5:12, kjv

Then Yeshua, the Son of God and the Son of Man, crowned King of kings and Lord of lords, arose having been fully arrayed in God's holy apparel mounted His magnificent white steed rode to earth in all His mighty glory.

And as He rode to the earth in all His glory, the angelic host, and the bride all were with Him. He is called Faithful and True, and in righteousness He judges and makes war. His eyes were as a flame of fire, and on His head were many crowns and He had a name written. His robe was dipped in blood and His name was The Word of God. His saints, which were in heaven, followed Him upon white horses; they were clothed in white and clean fine linen.

And a sharp sword went out of His mouth with which He could smite the nations and then rule them with a rod of iron. He tread upon the winepress of the fierceness and wrath of Almighty God because the nations did not believe and receive Him. They did not put their trust in Him as their Savior and Lord. He was patient and long-suffering with them. He loved and cared for them, but they would not freely give themselves over to Him in love. And He had a name written on His robe and on His thigh: King of Kings and Lord of Lords, as this was His Second Coming to earth.

As the light of His countenance pierced the darkness, the sky split apart and receded as a scroll when it is rolled up. Every mountain and island was moved out of its place.

Then the kings of the earth, the princes, generals, the rich, the mighty, and every slave and free man hid in caves among the rocks of the mountains. They called to the mountains and the rocks,

> Fall on us and hide us from the face of Him who sits on the throne and from the wrath of the Lamb! For the great day of their wrath has come, and who is able to stand?
>
> —Revelation 6:16

The nations who had set themselves against His people Yishrael were gathered together in the valley of Megiddo. Then I saw the beast and the kings of the earth and their armies gathered together to make war against the rider on the horse and His army. But the beast was captured and with him the false prophet who had deceived the people and had performed false miraculous signs.

I saw an angel come out of heaven, having the key to the Abyss and holding in his hand a great chain. He seized the dragon, that ancient serpent, who is the devil, or Satan, and bound him for a thousand years. He threw him into the Abyss and locked and sealed it over him, to keep him from deceiving the nations anymore until the thousand years were ended.

Someone shouted at the victory the Lord had won, saying,

> For he is the living God, and he will endure forever; His kingdom will never be destroyed and his rule will never end. He rescues and saves his people; he performs miraculous signs and wonders in the heavens and on earth.
>
> —Daniel 6:26–27, nlt

I then turned and saw Yeshua the King make His way to the great city Yerushalem on earth. It is written in the chronicles of old in the Book of Ezekiel chapter 46 that when the prince provides a free-will offering, a burnt offering or peace offering to the Lord, the gate facing the east shall be opened for him. It says, "And you shall provide a lamb a year old without blemish for a burnt offering to the LORD daily; morning by morning you shall provide it" (v. 13, NAS). In Ezekiel chapter 45 it says,

> It shall be the prince's part to provide the burnt offerings, the grain offerings and the drink offerings, at the feasts, on the new moons and on the Sabbaths, at all the appointed feasts of the house of Israel; he shall provide the sin offering, the grain offering, the burnt offering and the peace offerings, to make atonement for the house of Israel.
>
> —EZEKIEL 45:17, NAS

> The prince shall enter from the outside through the portico of the gateway and stand by the gatepost. The priests are to sacrifice his burnt offering and his fellowship offerings. He is to bow down in worship at the threshold of the gateway, then go out, but the gate will not be shut until evening. On the Sabbaths and New Moons the people of the land are to worship in the presence of the LORD at the entrance to that gateway.
>
> —EZEKIEL 46:2–3, NIV

As Yeshua made His way to the eastern gate that had been sealed up for over two thousand years, He spoke these words, saying,

> Lift up your heads, O you gates! And be lifted up, you everlasting doors! And the King of glory shall come in.
>
> —PSALM 24:7

Then I heard sounds coming from the earth saying, "Who is this king of glory?" (Ps. 24:8). The trees and the rocks responded, saying, "The LORD strong and mighty, The LORD mighty in battle" (v. 8).

Again, I heard Yeshua say,

Lift up your heads, O you gates! And be lifted up, you everlasting doors! And the King of glory shall come in.

—PSALM 24:9

Responding once again, I heard the earth answer back with,
"Who is this king of glory?" (Ps. 24:10). Then the birds of the air,
the trees, the rocks, and all of us who were standing with Him said,
"The LORD of hosts, He is the King of glory" (v. 10). When we said
this, the entrance that was sealed up fell apart and the eastern gate
was finally opened up and the great Prince entered His domain.

In the olden days when the prince entered this gate he brought
sacrifices and burnt offerings for the people as was stated before.
But this time the great Prince came in as the sacrifice. Yeshua had
already paid the price for the sins of the world.

It says in the Book of Isaiah, chapter 53:

Surely he took up our infirmities and carried our sorrows,
yet we considered him stricken by God, smitten by him and
afflicted. But he was pierced for our transgressions, he was
crushed for our iniquities; the punishment that brought us
peace was upon him, and by his wounds we are healed. We
all, like sheep, have gone astray, each of us has turned to his
own way, and the LORD has laid on him the iniquity of us all.

—ISAIAH 53:4–6, NIV

The cherubim who had previously lifted up their presence from
the great temple now rested themselves with their wings and their
wheels and they stood still within the holy of holies of the house of
the Lord, and the glory of the God of Yishrael hovered over them.

Yeshua would rule the present earth for a thousand years. After
the thousand year reign Satan rose up again to deceive the nations,
but Yeshua defeated him once and for all. Satan was put in the lake
of fire with those who did not repent would receive the second death.

In an instant the old earth and heavens were destroyed and
replaced with a new heaven and earth.

And I saw a new heaven and a new earth: for the first
heaven and the first earth were passed away; and there was
no more sea. And I John saw the holy city, new Jerusalem,

coming down from God out of heaven, prepared as a bride adorned for her husband. And I heard a great voice out of heaven, saying, Behold, the tabernacle of God is with men, and he will dwell with them, and they shall be his people, and God himself shall be with them, and be their God. And God shall wipe away all tears from their eyes; and there shall be no more death, neither sorrow, nor crying, neither shall there be any more pain: for the former things are passed away. And he that sat upon the throne said, Behold, I make all things new. And he said unto me, Write: for these words are true and faithful. And he said unto me, It is done. I am Alpha and Omega, the beginning and the end. I will give to him that is athirst of the fountain of the water of life freely. He that overcomes shall inherit all things; and I will be his God, and he shall be my son. But the fearful, and unbelieving, and the abominable, and murderers, and whoremongers, and sorcerers, and idolaters, and all liars, shall have their part in the lake which burns with fire and brimstone: which is the second death.

—REVELATION 21:1–8, KJV

Then an angel came.

He talked with me, saying, Come hither, I will shew you the bride, the Lamb's wife. And he carried me away in the spirit to a great and high mountain, and shewed me that great city, the holy Jerusalem, descending out of heaven from God, Having the glory of God: and her light *was* like unto a stone most precious, even like a jasper stone, clear as crystal. It had a wall great and high, *and* had twelve gates, and at the gates twelve angels, and names written thereon, which are *the names* of the twelve tribes of the children of Israel. On the east three gates; on the north three gates; on the south three gates; and on the west three gates. And the wall of the city had twelve foundations, and in them the names of the twelve apostles of the Lamb.

—REVELATION 21:9–14, KJV

As I looked, thrones were set in place, and the Ancient
of Days took his seat. His clothing was as white as snow,
the hair of His head was white as wool. His throne was
flaming with fire and its wheels were ablaze. A river of
fire was flowing, coming out before him. Thousands upon
thousands attended him, ten thousand times ten thousand
stood before Him. The court was seated and the books
were opened.

—DANIEL 7:9–10, NIV

As He sat upon the throne of His glory on earth and before
Him were gathered all people out of all nations; and He began to
separate them one from another, as a shepherd divides His sheep
from the goats. And He began to set the sheep on His right hand,
but the goats on the left. Then the King said unto them on His
right hand,

Come, you blessed of My Father, inherit the kingdom
prepared for you from the foundation of the world. For I
was hungry and you gave Me food; I was thirsty and you
gave Me drink; I was a stranger and you took Me in; I was
naked and you clothed Me; I was sick and you visited Me;
I was in prison and you came to Me.

—MATTHEW 25:34–36

Then the righteous answered Him, saying,

Lord, When did we see You hungry and feed You, or thirsty
and gave You drink? When did we see You a stranger and
take You in, or naked and clothe You? Or when did we see
You sick, or in prison, and came unto You?

—MATTHEW 25:37–39

And the King answered and said unto them,

Assuredly, I say unto you, inasmuch as you did it to one of
the least of these My brethren, you did it to Me.

—MATTHEW 25:40

Then He began to say also unto them on the left hand,

Depart from Me, you cursed, into everlasting fire prepared for the devil and his angels: For I was hungry and
you gave Me no food; I was thirsty and you gave Me no
drink; I was a stranger and you did not take me in; naked
and you did not clothe Me; sick and in prison and you did
not visit Me.

—Matthew 25:41–43

Then they answered Him, saying,

Lord, when did we see You hungry or thirsty or a
stranger or naked or sick or in prison, and did not minister to You?

—Matthew 25:44

Then He answered them, saying,

Assuredly, I say unto you, inasmuch as you did not do it to
one of the least of these, you did not do it to Me.

—Matthew 25:45

And these people will go away into everlasting punishment, but the righteous into eternal life.

—Matthew 25:46

[My Beloved] showed me a pure river of water of life,
clear as crystal, proceeding out of the throne of God
and of the Lamb. In the midst of the street of it, and on
either side of the river, was there the tree of life, which
bare twelve manner of fruits, and yielded her fruit every
month: and the leaves of the tree were for the healing of
the nations. And there shall be no more curse, but the
throne of God and of the Lamb shall be in it; and his servants shall serve him. And they shall see his face; and his
name shall be in their foreheads. And there shall be no
night there; and they need no candle, neither light of the
sun; for the Lord God giveth them light: and they shall
reign for ever and ever.

—Revelation 22:1–5, kjv

CHAPTER 23

YESHUA THE KING

⊘

Y ESHUA RECEIVED THE praise He so deserved.

After these things I looked, and behold, a great multitude which no one could number, from every nation and all tribes and peoples and tongues, standing before the throne and before the Lamb, clothed in white robes, and palm branches in their hands, and they cry out with a loud voice, saying, "Salvation to our God who sits on the throne, and to the Lamb!" All the angels were standing around the throne and around the elders and the four living creatures; and they fell on their faces before the throne and worshiped God, saying, "Amen, blessing and glory and wisdom, thanksgiving and honor and power and might, be to our God forever and ever. Amen."

—REVELATION 7:9–12, NAS

Then final words came forth as Yeshua turned and looked at the multitudes all around Him. He said to them,

He that has an ear, let him hear what the Spirit says to the churches: To him who overcomes I will give to eat from the tree of life, which is in midst of the Paradise of God....Be faithful until death, and I will give you the crown of life....He who overcomes shall not be hurt by the second death....To him that has overcome will I give some of the hidden manna to eat. And will give him a white stone, and on the stone a new name written which no man knows except him who receives it.

—REVELATION 2:7–10, 11, 17

> He who overcomes shall be clothed in white garments, and I will not blot out his name from the Book of Life; but I will confess his name before My Father and before His angels.
>
> —REVELATION 3:5

Again Yeshua spoke, saying,

> He who overcomes I will make him a pillar in the temple of My God, and he shall go out no more. I will write on him the name of My God and the name of the city of My God, the New Jerusalem, which comes down out of heaven from My God. And I will write upon him My new name.
>
> —REVELATION 3:12

Yeshua continued, saying,

> I counsel you to buy of Me gold tried in the fire, that you may be rich, and white raiment, that you may be clothed, and that the shame of your nakedness do not appear; and to anoint your eyes with eye salve, that you may see. As many as I love, I rebuke and chasten: be zealous therefore, and repent. Behold, I stand at the door, and knock: he who hears My voice, and opens the door, I will come in to him, and sup with him, and he with Me. To him who overcomes I grant to sit with Me in My throne, even as I also overcame, and am set down with My Father in His throne. He who has an ear, let him hear what the Spirit says unto the churches.
>
> —REVELATION 3:18–22

Finally Yeshua said,

> Behold, I come quickly; and My reward is with Me, to give every one according to his work. I am Alpha and Omega, the Beginning and the End, the First and the Last....I am the Root and the Offspring of David, and the Bright and Morning Star.....Blessed are those who do [My] commandments, that they may have right to the tree of life, and

may enter in through the gates into the city.... And the
Spirit and the bride say, "Come!" And let him who hears
say, "Come!" And let him who thirsts come. Whoever
desires, let him take the water of life freely.... Surely I
come quickly!

                              —REVELATION 22:12–13, 16, 14, 17, 20

PERSONAL INVITATION

I F YOU WOULD like to have a love relationship like this, then call upon the Messiah Yeshua, Isa, Jesus, the Anointed One, the Son of God. Simply repeat this prayer:

> *O God of Abraham, Isaac, and Jacob, I have heard the salvation message of how Messiah Yeshua, Isa, Jesus, Your Son, died for me and took all my sins upon Himself for me so that I might be forgiven and pardoned through His shed blood.*
>
> *Messiah Yeshua (Jesus, Isa), I ask You to forgive me of all of my sins, and to come into my heart, and to live out Your life on the inside of me. I totally commit my life to You, and give You this vessel for Your use.*
>
> *Now I ask You to send the Holy Spirit of God to fill and empower me so I can be bold for You. Holy Spirit, I receive You now.*
>
> *O God in heaven, now that Messiah Yeshua (Jesus, Isa) has come into my heart, I understand that I am now Your child and You are now my Father. Father, I thank You for saving me and for Your precious Holy Spirit who dwells in me now. Thank You in the precious name of Messiah Yeshua (Jesus, Isa). Amen!*

If you have received Messiah Yeshua, Isa, Jesus, as your personal Lord and Savior and He has empowered you with the Holy Spirit and you want to enjoy an intimate relationship with Him, then pray this prayer:

> *O heavenly Father, I desire that deep intimate relationship with Messiah Yeshua (Jesus, Isa). Your Word says that the*

Holy Spirit knows all things, and by my asking He will reveal the presence of Messiah Yeshua (Jesus, Isa) to me. I ask You, Holy Spirit, whom I speak to as my best friend, please reveal Yeshua (Jesus, Isa) to me in a more personal and intimate way. In the name of Messiah Yeshua (Jesus, Isa), I thank You for doing this. Amen.

PART I: THE JOURNEY

❧

Chapter 1

Jeremiah 31:3; Revelation 3:20; Isaiah 41:18; Romans 8:37, 1; Matthew 5:6; Acts 4:12; John 14:26; Acts 2:1–4; Deuteronomy 31:6; John 2:1–10; John 5:19; Luke 7:36–38, 44–50; Luke 9:51–56; Matthew 26:17–68; 27:11–66; Ephesians 4:8–9; Psalm 8:4–6; Genesis 3:15; Revelation 1:18; Acts 3:19; Luke 4:1–13; John 20:1–18; Matthew 28; Psalm 8:4–6; Acts 1:1–11; Romans 5; Isaiah 53:1–12; John 14:26; Hebrews 13:5; Joshua 1:9; Psalm 51; Ezekiel 14:3; 2 Chronicles 14:2–5; 1 Kings 18:21–39; Isaiah 35:1–10; Philippians 4:19; Galatians 5:6; Genesis 26:18; 1 Corinthians 12:4–10; 1 John 4:18; James 4:7–8; Isaiah 61:10; John 10:10

Chapter 2

Song of Solomon 6:3; Psalm 91; Psalm 18; Psalm 23; Song of Solomon 1:2; Psalm 72:19; John 14:2–3; Ephesians 4:26; John 6:48; Isaiah 53:3–5; Mark 16:15–18; Psalm 1:3; Matt. 7:17; Galatians 5:22–23; Matthew 18:11; Romans 6:23

Chapter 3

2 Corinthians 11:13–15; Obadiah 1:3–4; 1 John 2:15–17; Romans 3:23; 2 Corinthians 4:4; Ezekiel 28:12–19; Isaiah 14:12–17; Luke 22:42; Hebrews 7:17; 9:11–15, 24–28; 10:9–14, 24–28; 5:5–10

Chapter 4

Song of Solomon 4:12; Romans 8:1; 3:22; Revelation 4:6–13; Revelation 12:10–11; Ephesians 2:4–10; Revelation 12:10; Ephesians 6:10–18; 6:14; Psalm 117:2; John 14:6; 17:17; Matthew 7:24–27; Psalm 40:11b; Ephesians 6:12–13; Psalm 51:6; 1 Peter 1:13; Hebrews 13:5; 1 John 2:12; John 8:32; John 14:6; Ephesians 4:22–25; Ephesians 4:14–16; John 4:24; Colossians 3:8–10; Psalm

91:4; Psalm 119:142; Proverbs 10:2; Proverbs 12:28; Philippians 3:9;
Galatians 3:10–12; Isaiah 64:6: II Corinthians 5:21; John 6:46–58;
Romans 3:23–26; Romans 5:8–10; Exodus 28:15–21; Ephesians
1:3–7; 1 Kings 3:9; Jeremiah 23:6; Romans 10:4; 2 Corinthians
5:21; Romans 8:10; 1 Corinthians 1:30; Psalm 94:15; Isaiah
64:6; Ephesians 6:15; Romans 5:1–2; Proverbs 4:26–27; Psalm
118:13–14; Isaiah 52:6–7; Romans 10:15; Ephesians 6:16; Jeremiah
46:3–4; Psalm 18:39–40, 45, 47–48; Hebrews 11:1, 3, 6, 33–34;
1 Thessalonians 5:8–9; Habakkuk 2:4; Romans 10:17; Ephesians
6:17; 1 Corinthians 15:1–2; 1 Thessalonians 5:8–9; Psalm 140:6–7;
1 Corinthians 2:16; Philippians 2:5–11; Ephesians 4:20–25; 1 Peter
4:1–2; 2 Corinthians 10:3–5; Ephesians 4:14; Colossians 2:13–15;
1 Timothy 6:15; Romans 8:5–9; Ephesians 6:17; John 1:1–5; Isaiah
49:2; Psalm 149:4–9; Hebrews 4:12; James 4:6–8; Zechariah
4:6; Deuteronomy 20:3–4; Psalm 18:32–36; Jeremiah 46:3–4;
Philippians 2:9–11; Luke 10:19; Ephesians 1:18; Ephesians 4:32;
Colossians 3:13; Isaiah 53:3–5; John 10:11–18

Chapter 5

2 Timothy 1:7; Mark 16:15–18; John 10:10; Luke 10:19–20;
Philippians 2:9–12; Song of Solomon 4:16; 1:2–3; 6:9; 8:6–7

Chapter 6

Psalm 91:1–2; Song of Solomon 2:14; Psalm 107:29–30; Matthew
8:23–26; Psalm 62:6; Song of Solomon 2:8–9; Psalm 59:9; Exodus
15:2; Psalm 28:7; 118:14; Job 12:13; Psalm 27:1; Song of Solomon
2:10–14; Jeremiah 1:5; Psalm 138:3; Proverbs 10:29; Exodus 19:4;
Psalm 103:5; Isaiah 40:29–31

Chapter 7

Psalm 27:5; Hebrews 4:1–16; Song of Solomon 5:10–16; Ezekiel
43:2; Revelation 22:1; Ezekiel 47:1–12; John 7:37–38; Song of
Solomon 4:12; Psalm 1:1–13; John 14:2–3; Revelation 19:7–8;
21:2; 22:17; Song of Solomon 2:3–4; Jeremiah 31:12–13; Song of
Solomon 4:12–16; Ezekiel 36:35; Jeremiah 31:3; Psalm 34:1–2;
71:6; 119:164; 95:6–7; 42:1–2; Song of Solomon 1:2–4; 2:3–5;
Psalm 23:1–4; Isaiah 58:11; Revelation 12:11; 2 Corinthians 5:7;

Isaiah 58:12; 1 Corinthians 15:51–52; Matthew 22:2–14; Revelation 12:7–11; Proverbs 2:1–13

Chapter 8

Psalm 34:4; 2 Timothy 1:7; 1 Samuel 30:6; 2 Corinthians 12:9, Matthew 25:20–23; Romans 5:20; 3:23–26; John 1:17, Song of Solomon 2:9; Psalm 126:5–6; Isaiah 12:3–6; 35:1–10; 51:11; Psalm 30:5; Nehemiah 8:10; John 1:12; Revelation 14:15–16; John 4:35; Song of Solomon 7:11–13; Joel 3:13; Matthew 9:37–38; Genesis 15:1; Luke 10:2; Mark 4:26–29; Psalm 91; Proverbs 3:5–6; 1 Samuel 17:47; Isaiah 54:5; 2 Timothy 1:7; Psalm 55:16–19a; Romans 8:28; 1 John 4:18–19, Galatians 5:6; Hebrews 11:6; Psalm 99:9; Revelation 19:7; 2:4–5

Chapter 9

Romans 8:1–2; Psalm 34:4; Ezekiel 47:1–12; Ephesians 5:25–27; Song of Solomon 2:2, 14; 1:9–11; 2:3, 4–9, 10–13, 16–17; Psalm 22:3; Matthew 21:16; Song of Solomon 2:10–13; 1:4; 1 Corinthians 6:19–20

PART II: ABIDING IN THE SECRET PLACE

Chapter 10

Song of Solomon 1:13–14; 2:1–17; 4:1–16; 2:8–17; Revelation 21:9–14; John 15:1–10; 7:16–18; Psalm 119:103–104; 19:9–11; Song of Solomon 5:1; Genesis 1:16–17; Psalm 8:3; Colossians 1:13–20; John 5:19–23; 4:35–38; Mark 4:26–29; Psalm 46:4; Revelation 7:9; Song of Solomon 4:9–11; Isaiah 55:8–9; Song of Solomon 2:13; 4:12–15; John 15:1–2; Song of Solomon 5:1; Romans 8:29; Hebrews 9:11–15; 2 Corinthians 6:16–18; Romans 12:2; 2 Corinthians 3:18; Romans 8:29; 12:1; 1 Corinthians 6:19–20; Psalm 12:6–7; Song of Solomon 4:9–11; Psalm 19:10; John 10:10; Matthew 9:17; 1 Peter 1:8; 2:1–2; Song of Solomon 1:15; 4:1; 2 Corinthians 3:18; John 1:14;

Song of Solomon 4:1, 11, 15; 5:1; Psalm 27:1; Isaiah 40:31; Psalm 144:2; 22:3; Isaiah 11:9; 60:1–3; John 16:33

Chapter 11

Matthew 7:17–19; Psalm 24:1–2; Joel 3:2, 11–18; Zechariah 14:1–11; Isaiah 41:15–16; Micah 4:13; Matthew 13:8; Nehemiah 8:10; Exodus 38; Leviticus 16; Revelation 3:18; Hebrews 1:13; Revelation 1:12–16; 4:5; Zechariah 4:2–6; Leviticus 24:5–8; John 6:48–51; Joshua 5:13–15; Zechariah 3:1–10; John 6:53; Romans 3:23–26; Ephesians 5:25–27; 2:13–18; Hebrews 4:14–16, 6–10; 7:17; Revelation 4:8; 2 Chronicles 5:11–14; Psalm 149:5–9; Revelation 1:12–18; 19:11–13; 7:17; Galatians 4:19; 2 Timothy 3:12; Nehemiah 8:10; Psalm 1:1–3; 92:15; Ephesians 5:20; Zechariah 4:6–10; Psalm 149:1–3; John 4:13–14; Revelation 7:17; Matthew 11:12; 2 Timothy 1:7; Luke 10:19; Jeremiah 31:3; 1 Corinthians 2:16; Psalm 91; Colossians 2:11–15; Philippians 2:9–11; Hebrews 12:1–2; Psalm 34:4; John 15:1–8; 16:33; Revelation 17:14; 5:5–14

Chapter 12

Isaiah 40:21–23; Ephesians 1:3–4; 1:17–23; Luke 10:18–19; Habakkuk 2:4; Ephesians 1:18; Numbers 22:41; Deuteronomy 28:1–13; Numbers 24:8–9; Exodus 3:1–6; Numbers 24:14–16; Revelation 4:1; Numbers 33:51–53; Deuteronomy 33:26–29; 28:1–2; 32:11–13; Ezekiel 3:17; Ephesians 6:18; Ezekiel 33:3–9; 3:18–19; Isaiah 52:7–10; Jeremiah 31:6; 51:12; John 14:26; Proverbs 3:5–6

Chapter 13

John 8:44; 10:10; Joshua 1:6–9; 2 Corinthians 10:4–5; Micah 7:7–8; Luke 4:18; Nahum 3:10–14; Philippians 4:13; 2 Corinthians 10:4–5; John 8:31–32; 1 Peter 2:24–25; Isaiah 53:1–12; Jeremiah 48:41–42; Luke 4:8; 1 Peter 5:5; Proverbs 3:5–6; Jeremiah 31:3; Romans 8:35–39; Psalm 18:1–3; 32:7; Nahum 1:7; Jeremiah 16:19; Micah 5:11–15; Luke 4:8; Ruth 3:4; John 10:10; 2 Timothy 1:7; Jeremiah 29:11; 31:3; Deuteronomy 31:8; Jeremiah 16:19; Luke 10:19; 2 Timothy 1:7; 1 Corinthians 2:16; Philippians 4:8; Psalm 18:1–19; John 8:32

Chapter 14

Philippians 4:6–8; John 16:7–15; Deuteronomy 32:8–14; Exodus 19:4–6; Psalm 91:11–12; Isaiah 41:9–16; Deuteronomy 33:25–26, 12, 27–29; Psalm 18:37–48; 91:4; Luke 10:19; Deuteronomy 32:11; Job 39:27–29; Jeremiah 49:22; Habakkuk 1:8; Lamentations 4:19; Isaiah 40:28–31; 40:3–5; 64:6; Jeremiah 29:11; Matthew 5:6; Isaiah 40:5; 40:9–11; Jeremiah 51:20–21; Ephesians 6:12; Galatians 5:22–23; 2 Corinthians 10:4

Chapter 15

John 3:5–8; 14:9–11; 1 Peter 5:8–11; 2 Corinthians 10:4–5; Colossians 2:15; Isaiah 55:11; Ephesians 6:10–12; Isaiah 54:17; Ephesians 6:13–15; 4:14; 6:16–18; 1:17–23; Revelation 12:11; 13:8; Joshua 5:13–15; Judges 4; 5; 5:12; Joshua 6; Judges 6:11–16, 34; 7:1–25; 2 Samuel 23:8–10; 1 Samuel 30:1–20, 8; 2 Samuel 5:17–25; Acts 12:1–17; 16:16–34; John 1:23; 6:37; 2 Peter 3:9; John 10:10; Matthew 11:28–30

Chapter 16

Revelation 1:13–16; Matthew 24:4–14, 27, 29–31, 23–24, 36–42, 44–51; Ephesians 6:12; Psalm 27:1–8, 11; Ephesians 3:16; 6:10–13, 18; Luke 10:19; Ephesians 6:14; 4:15; 6:14–17; 1 Peter 5:8; Matthew 25:14–30, 29–31, 13; 24:27–36; John 14:6; 2 Kings 6:16–17; Ephesians 6:18

Chapter 17

2 Corinthians 10:4–6; Isaiah 54:17; Romans 13:11–14; Ephesians 5:6–17; 1 Thessalonians 5:1–11; Jeremiah 22:7–9; Revelation 2:2–3; Matthew 24:42–44; Revelation 16:15; Matthew 25:1–13; Isaiah 62:6–7; Exodus 12:23; Revelation 11:3–12; Jeremiah 22:7–9; Revelation 3:10; Ezekiel 8:12–16; 9:1–11; Revelation 7:1–3; 9:4–5; Ezekiel 9:5–11; Revelation 12:7–12, 13–17; Hebrews 13:5–6; 9:11–14; Romans 8:37

Chapter 18

Matthew 25:1–13; Esther 2:3; Revelation 19:7–8; Ephesians 5:25–27; Psalm 45:9–15; 1 Thessalonians 5:2; Song of Solomon 1:2–4; 2:4–6; 1:3; Revelation 21:9–14

Chapter 19

Matthew 22:2–14; Luke 14:16–24; Song of Solomon 2:4, 16, 5–6; Genesis 49:11–12; Matthew 26:29, 26–28; Psalm 18:34, 7–19; 34:1; Romans 8:35–39

Chapter 20

Revelation 19:6–9; Psalm 68:24–25; 45:2, 6–9, 13–15, 17; Song of Solomon 1:15–16; 4:1, 10–13, 12–15, 7–10; Psalm 45:17; Song of Solomon 5:10–16

Chapter 21

Song of Solomon 2:4; Genesis 2:21–24; John 19:33–34; Revelation 22:1–5; Zephaniah 3:14–20; Micah 4:7–8

Chapter 22

Song of Solomon 5:10–16; Revelation 1:13–16, 5:9–12; Philippians 2:10–11; Isaiah 45:23; 9:6–7; Revelation 4:8–11; Isaiah 6:3; Matthew 3:17; Revelation 19:11–16; 4:3–4, 10–11; 5:1–2, 6–12; 19:6–16; 6:12–17; 19:19–21; 20:1–3; Daniel 6:26–27; Ezekiel 46:1–3, 12–15; 45:17; 46:2–3 Psalm 24:7–10; Isaiah 53:1–12; Ezekiel 10:15–19; Revelation 20:7–10; 21:1–14; Daniel 7:9–14, 18; Matthew 25:31–46; Revelation 22:1–5

Chapter 23

Revelation 7:9–12; 2:1–7, 8–11, 12–17; 3:1–5, 5–13; 12, 18–22; 22:12–13, 16, 14, 17, 20–21; Ezekiel 47:6–12

THE SECRET PLACE:

THE GARDEN
OF LOVE

TEACHING AND STUDY GUIDE

THE SECRET PLACE TEACHING AND STUDY GUIDE

CHAPTER 1: JUST FRIENDS

I N ORDER TO receive the most out of this book the Lord Yeshua has put together this teaching and study guide to help guide you into the deeper things of the Spirit.

Yeshua, the Lord, wants to have a deep intimate relationship with each believer, for He is the lover of our souls. In Revelation 3:20 Jesus stands at the door of your heart and knocks. Will you let Him in?

The Word of God says in Matthew 5:6, "Blessed are those who hunger and thirst for righteousness, for they shall be filled." It is important to have a quiet time with the Lord; to pray daily and develop that special time with Yeshua. Tell Him everything; how you feel, your dreams and aspirations, and especially that you love Him.

As you spend time with Yeshua, keep a written diary or journal. You can express your love for Him with a love letter, a poem, or a song. Just pour out your heart to Him. Even if you are feeling bad or angry, tell Him how you feel. King David did this in the psalms. Take time to read the psalms and see that David shared everything with the Lord God. Be sure and write in your diary or journal every day.

As you go through this study guide, also read Song of Solomon in your Bible. You will find it in the Old Testament after Proverbs and Ecclesiastes. Song of Solomon contains love songs and has only eight chapters. Song of Solomon is the story of Solomon the shepherd/king and his love relationship with a young Shulamite girl who is his bride. Song of Solomon is also the story of Christ's (Yeshua) love for His church individually and as a whole. As you read it you will see the similarities.

Chapter 1, "Just Friends" begins at first meeting. Write down in a few words how you came to know the Lord Jesus (Yeshua).

_____

_____

_____

_____

How did you feel when He came into your heart?

_____

_____

_____

If you were not born again before you read this book, did reading this book change your mind about God, your heavenly Father, His Son, Jesus (Yeshua), and His Holy Spirit? Explain:

_____

_____

_____

_____

Did you understand the gospel message about Jesus (Yeshua) dying on the cross for you?

Yes _____

No _____

If you have come from a difficult past and don't feel you can be forgiven, know that the blood of Jesus (Yeshua) is greater than any sin. Please read Luke 7:36–50. Notice verses 42 and 43 where it points out the sinner with the greatest debt had the greatest love.

One evening when you are alone or in your prayer closet, put on some soft worship music or just sing a love song from your heart.

Then, just like the woman with the alabaster box, pour out your love and tears of gratitude and wash the Master's feet.

We as Christians at salvation begin a journey with our Savior. It is a journey of love resulting in growth and change. Our Lord does not expect maturity from us at the beginning. Just like a parent doesn't expect a baby who is just learning to crawl, to run a race, the Lord doesn't expect us to walk in total Christlikeness in the beginning nor does He expect us to know deep spiritual things either. We are all growing in grace and faith.

Our spirit is born again, but our mind and heart, our soul, must change and be renewed. The old nature must die so that Christ's nature might live. It's a process, from glory to glory. Please read John 12:23–26. In verse 24 Jesus (Yeshua) says, "Most assuredly, I say to you, unless a grain of wheat falls into the ground and dies, it remains alone, but if it dies, it produces much grain [fruit]."

The process of dying begins with His removing our idols one by one. Idols are things we love more than God. What I mean by removing idols of the heart does not necessarily mean that God is going to remove a person from your life, if you idolize that person. He will open your eyes so that you will see that person through the eyes of truth. As you draw closer to Jesus (Yeshua), your eyes will be upon Him and Him alone, then you won't have idolatry for others or things and you will be much happier for it.

List a few areas in your heart which you use to fill a void in your own life, such as food, clothes, or other people. Be truthful.

_____

_____

_____

_____

Read Genesis 35:4–5. When they put away their idols, the fear of God came upon their enemies and they walked right through.

The Lord asks you to bring these things to Him, give them to Him, confess and ask for forgiveness and repent (desire to turn away from). Remember, this is a journey with the Lord. You may have to do this more than once. It's Jesus' righteousness in us that we depend on, not our own. It's His righteousness that causes us to walk in victory.

We all have some form of fear in our lives that we have to deal with. Some fears may be obvious and others may be more subtle. List some fears that you might have. Examples would be the "fear of man" or "fear of the dark."

_____

_____

_____

_____

After listing your fears, take this list before the Lord and confess and renounce and forsake each fear. Receive His forgiveness, and then ask the Lord for grace to face these fears and walk through all of them. The Word of God says He has delivered me out of all my fears (Ps. 34:4).

Jesus (Yeshua) will take you on a journey out of all your fears. You will be amazed when you see yourself doing things in victory that you couldn't do before.

Look up these scriptures and fill in the blanks:

2 Timothy 1:7: "For God has not given us a spirit of _____, but of _____, _____, and _____."

Psalm 34:4: "I sought the LORD, and He _____ me, And _____ me from all my fears."

1 John 4:16: "And we have known and believed the _____ that God has for us. God is _____, and he who _____ in love _____ in God, and God in him."

1 John 4:18–19: "There is no _____ in love; but _____ love casts out _____, because _____ involves torment. But he who _____ has not been made _____ in love. We _____ Him because He _____ loved us."

THE SECRET PLACE TEACHING AND STUDY GUIDE

Chapter 2: True Love

As you go through difficult or stressful times, remember that you are moving closer to Him. If you *praise Him and release thanksgiving* while going through trials, most of the time the trials will be shorter. But if you gripe and complain in the midst of them, just like the children of Israel stayed in the wilderness forty years, you will too, but hopefully not forty years. Their time in the wilderness was only supposed to last forty days, but because of griping and complaining, their wilderness experience was multiplied back to them. Be quick to confess sin and repent and be restored.

In the space below write your own praises and thanksgiving to the Lord:

_____

_____

_____

_____

Even in the midst of griping and complaining, if you will repent and run to Him, He will forgive you and hide you in the secret place as you walk through the wilderness. Our Father is working His character within you. He is removing the works of the flesh, the trees of unrighteousness, and replacing them with His trees of righteousness.

As you walk through trials, be sure you give your emotions to Him. Some of the negative emotions the works of the flesh bring forth are fear, doubt, worry, anger, strife, bitterness, resentment, unforgiveness, and unbelief (See Galatians 5:16–21, 26). These keep you from walking in the emotions of the Lord which are love, joy, peace, and other fruit of the Spirit (Gal. 5:22–25). When you find yourself walking in negative emotions, call out to Jesus (Yeshua) for help and He will come to your aid immediately.

Make a list of some negative emotions in your own life and find a fruit of the Spirit from Galatians 5:22–23 that you want to replace it. Then find scriptures to confirm this.

Examples: Replace fear with love: 2 Timothy 1:7; 1 John 4:18–19.

_____

_____

_____

_____

Jeremiah 31:3 says, "I have loved you with an everlasting love; Therefore with lovingkindness I have drawn you." God's love is greater than all our sins.

Through all these trials you will be made perfect in His love. In each of these trials, run to the Lord; find comforting love in Him. You will then be made perfect in His love, for perfect love casts out all fear (1 John 4:18). First Corinthians 13:1–13 tells us what true and perfect love is.

THE SECRET PLACE TEACHING AND STUDY GUIDE

CHAPTER 3: THE DECEIVER

HAVE YOU EVER found yourself in a difficult situation because *you wanted to do it your way and didn't ask the Lord for wisdom?* Be quick and run to the Lord; confess and repent and receive His forgiveness, mercy, and grace.

Or is the enemy (Satan) trying to deceive you or seduce you into compromising your faith? Run to Jesus (Yeshua's) arms, confess, and repent. You will find shelter. Yeshua will strengthen you to press on through. Wisdom for overcoming the tempter or deceiver is in Matthew 4:1–11. Read that scripture and stand on God's Word.

Look up the following scriptures and fill in the blanks:

Matthew 6:33: "But seek _____ the kingdom of God and His _____, and all these things will be added to you."

Jeremiah 31:3: "The Lord has appeared of old to me, saying: 'Yes, I have _____ you with an _____ love; Therefore with _____ I have drawn you.'"

Proverbs 10:12: "Hatred stirs up _____, But _____ covers all sins."

1 Peter 4:8: "And above all things have fervent _____ for one another, for '_____ will cover a multitude of _____.'"

Romans 5:8: "But God demonstrates His own _____ toward us, in that while we were still _____, Christ _____ for us."

Matthew 4:4: "But He answered and said, 'It is written, "Man shall not live by _____ alone, but by every _____ that proceeds from the _____ of God"'" (Deut. 8:3).

Matthew 4:7: "Jesus said unto him, 'It is written again, "You shall not _____ the LORD your God"'" (Deut. 6:16).

Matthew 4:10: "Then Jesus said to him, 'Away with you, Satan! For it is written, "You shall _____ the LORD your God, and Him only you shall _____ "'" (Deut. 6:13).

When the tempter (the deceiver) comes, he will come sometimes with flattering words that pull on the pride of the listener. If the words cause you to be puffed up or think more highly of yourself that you ought to (Rom. 12:3; 1 Tim. 3:6), be on guard; because the devil is as a roaring lion seeking those he might devour (1 Pet. 5:8).

THE SECRET PLACE TEACHING AND STUDY GUIDE

CHAPTER 4: THE GARDEN
(WISDOM ABOUT THE BATTLE)

As YOU GO through trials in your life remember Yeshua (Jesus) is with you, leading and guiding you. You are not alone. Yeshua is drawing you closer to Himself as you go through the fire. His purpose is to draw you to His garden, the secret place.

In the garden He wants to share His most intimate secrets with you. His garden is the place where He shares His revelation. He will give you His wisdom about the battles you face in your life.

Look up the Scripture in Ephesians 6:10–18 and fill in the blanks:

Finally, my brethren, be _____ in the Lord and the power of His _____. Put on the whole _____ of God, that you may be able to _____ against the _____ of the devil. For we do not _____ against flesh and blood, but against principalities, against _____, against the _____ of the darkness of this age, against spiritual hosts of _____ in the _____ places. Therefore take up the _____ armor of God, that you may be able to _____ in the _____ day, and having done all, to stand. Stand therefore, having girded your _____ with _____, having put on the _____ of _____, and having shod your _____ with the _____ of the gospel of _____; above all, taking the _____ of _____ with which you will be able to _____ all the fiery _____ of the _____ one. And take the _____ of _____ and the _____ of the _____, which is the _____ of _____; praying always with all _____ and _____ in the Spirit, being _____ to this end with all perseverance and _____ for all the _____.

Put on the armor of God every day. Realize that Yeshua, the Christ, is your armor. He is your righteousness, your shield, and your exceedingly great reward (Gen. 15:1). Yeshua is the Word that causes the enemy to retreat in your mind and in your life. Yeshua came to bring life and life more abundantly (John 10:10).

Jesus is the King of glory, strong and mighty in battle. Fill in the blanks for this scripture in Psalm 24:8, 10:

> Who is this _____ of glory? The Lord _____ and mighty, The Lord _____ in battle.... Who is this King of _____? The Lord of _____, He is the King of _____.

The Lord is great, and Jesus has given us the victory. Fill in the blanks for this scripture in 1 Chronicles 29:11–12:

> Yours, O Lord, is the greatness, The _____ and the _____, The _____ and the _____; For all that is in _____ and in earth is _____; Yours is the _____, O Lord, And you are _____ as _____ over all, Both _____ and _____ come from You, And You _____ over all. In Your hand is _____ and _____; In Your _____ it is to make _____ And to give _____ to all.

Read Colossians 2:14–15 and fill in the blanks for verse 15:

> [God] having disarmed _____ and _____, He made a public _____ of them, _____ over them in it [the Cross].

Jesus stripped Satan of his authority and gave it to us (the body of Christ) when He said, "I have given you authority and power...over all the power that the enemy [possesses], and nothing shall in any way harm you" (Luke 10:19, AMPC).

THE SECRET PLACE TEACHING AND STUDY GUIDE

CHAPTER 5: UP THE MOUNTAIN

AS WE COME closer to Yeshua, Jesus, He takes us on different levels of the revelation of His presence. We must first walk by faith knowing that Jesus is near because the Word says so. But there comes a time in our faith walk that Yeshua will allow His presence to be felt and seen. The tangible presence of the mantle of His anointing can be physically felt. This is called going up the mountain and experiencing His presence. Jesus Christ's presence can be felt on earth and He can be seen in the heavenly realms with the eyes of your spirit, also known as the eyes of your imagination. Then finally, when He is ready He will allow Himself to be seen with your natural eyes.

If we will press into Him in prayer, praise, and worship, He will begin to reveal Himself. To start your journey to meet with the Lord, begin meditating on scriptures about people that have already seen Him. Look at these scriptures: Isaiah 6:1–8; Ezekiel 1:3–28 (particularly verses 26–28); Daniel 7:9–14; 10:5–6; Revelation 1:10–18; 4:1–11.

To begin this quest you must start by communicating with Yeshua as Adam and Eve communicated with the Father God in the Garden of Eden. A good way to begin speaking to Yeshua is to write Him a love letter, poem, or a song. Below write a love letter or a song expressing your deepest love for Him. You may use scriptures from the Song of Solomon to express yourself.

_____

_____

_____

_____

THE SECRET PLACE TEACHING AND STUDY GUIDE

CHAPTER 6: IN THE MIDST OF THE STORM

As you come to maturity, you will find that as the storms rage all around you have nothing to fear. When the storms come, run to the One who calms the storms. Read Matthew 8:23–27; Mark 4:35–41; Luke 8:22–25.

Think of a past storm in your life. Did you overcome with the Word or did the storm overcome you? Write down some of your experiences.

_____

_____

_____

_____

Can you think of some scriptures that you can stand on to help you overcome? Ask the Lord Yeshua for scriptures to stand on. For example: if you have trouble with fear, you can confess and stand on 2 Timothy 1:7. Write them here:

_____

_____

_____

_____

Are you standing on the solid rock or on shifting sand? See Matthew 7:24–27 and Luke 6:46–49. Are you putting your trust in and obeying the Word?

In Song of Solomon 2:9 it talks about Solomon showing Himself through the lattice. In Song of Solomon, Solomon represents Jesus our Lord. In this verse the word *lattice* represents trials or storms. In other words, storms come into your life only so that God (Jesus, our Beloved) can show Himself strong on your behalf (2 Chron. 16:9). After the storm things become clearer and you move to a new level of faith and you move closer to the Lord.

Can you think of a storm or trial where Yeshua showed Himself in the midst of your life? Did you see the Lord in a deeper light? Write your story down and how you saw Yeshua for who He was revealing Himself as (for example: healer, provider, shepherd, etc.)

_____

_____

_____

_____

_____

_____

THE SECRET PLACE TEACHING AND STUDY GUIDE

CHAPTER 7: TOUCHING THE SECRET PLACE

THE SECRET PLACE is the place of intimacy with the Lord. It's the place of your prayer closet. It's the place where it's you and Yeshua sharing your innermost secrets with each other.

When there is a storm or a trial where do you run? Do you run to Him when you are emotionally hurt or wounded? Or do you go to the television, eat food, or buy something? Why not take it to Yeshua? Tell Him how you feel, even if you are angry at something or someone. Yeshua will listen, and He will comfort you. Don't be afraid to tell Him how you feel. He wants to reveal those hidden secret things about Himself to you. Tell Him how much you love Him. Worship Him! Then He will tell you wonderful things about yourself. He will speak healing love words to you and bring you the emotional healing that you need, so you can forgive the other person.

Know that you are His beloved bride and He has something wonderful to give you. You will find out who you are as you sit and bask in His presence.

Write a short description of what Yeshua looks like to you:

_____

_____

_____

Now write a short paragraph of what He means to you:

_____

_____

_____

_____

THE SECRET PLACE TEACHING AND STUDY GUIDE

CHAPTER 8: HE DELIVERS ME FROM ALL MY FEARS

PLEASE ANSWER THESE questions about yourself. Be truthful.

1. When you are in a trial do you have trouble with fear? _____

2. In the midst of a trial are you able to praise God?
   _____

3. When your prayers seemingly don't get answered, do you still love and praise God? _____
   _____

4. Or do you get angry and withdraw from Him and His love? _____

You can get angry with Him. God appreciates your being honest with Him. But remember, He said He would never ever leave you or forsake you (Heb. 13:5). God always keeps His Word. Remember, when you are angry, run to God, not to things or people. When the enemy (fear) comes in like a flood, the Lord will raise up a standard against him (Isa 59:19).

Read Psalm 91. Second Timothy 1:7 tells us: "For God has not given us a spirit of fear, but of power and love and of a sound mind."

1. Are you training yourself to stand on God's Word?
   _____

God is not a liar, what He said He will do, He will do (Num. 23:19).

Read Matthew 8:23–27.

And He said to them, Why are you timid and afraid, O you of little faith? Then He got up and rebuked the winds and the sea, and there was a great and wonderful calm

(a perfect peaceableness). And the men were stunned with
bewildered wonder and marveled, saying, What kind of
man is this that even the winds and sea obey Him!

—MATTHEW 8:26–27, AMPC

Write in the space below other scriptures that you would stand
on in the midst of a storm.

_____

_____

_____

_____

Write a brief story of a storm you went through and how God
brought you through.

_____

_____

_____

_____

THE SECRET PLACE TEACHING AND STUDY GUIDE

CHAPTER 9: HE IS MY JOY (THE RIVER OF LIFE)

PLEASE ANSWER THESE questions about yourself.

1. When you are spending time with the Lord do you sit quietly and wait for Him to speak? _____

2. Or do you talk all the time? _____

After quietly waiting for Him, write down something the Lord has said or revealed to you. It may be an impression or an audible voice, or He may give you a scripture or put a picture in your mind. Write what He gives you on the following lines.

_____

_____

_____

_____

Read in Song of Solomon. It's located after Proverbs in the Old Testament. Let the Holy Spirit sing a new song to you. When you hear the words, write it down. Then sing a song back to Him. It can be spontaneous or may come from a psalm. Write a love song to the Lord. Feel the Lord's arms around you as you sing your song, and then write it on the following lines.

_____

_____

_____

_____

THE SECRET PLACE TEACHING AND STUDY GUIDE

CHAPTER 10: SPENDING TIME WITH HIM

WHAT CHARACTERISTICS DO you see in Yeshua (Jesus) that are also in His Father God?

For a clue look in the New Testament books of Matthew, Mark, Luke, and John. You may want to write down the scriptures as you find them. Write as many as you can think of on the following lines.

_____

_____

_____

_____

Read Galatians 5:13–26. Write down a list on the following lines of the work of the flesh and compare with the work of the Spirit (fruit). Notice that the fruit of love will overtake several works of the flesh.

Work of the Flesh

_____

_____

_____

_____

Work of the Holy Spirit

_____

_____

_____

_____

Now read 1 Corinthians 13:1–13. "But the greatest of these is *love*" (v. 13, emphasis added). When you surrender to Christ Jesus' love and allow Him to flow through you, the Holy Spirit will produce the fruit of the Spirit within you, which will overtake the works of the flesh.

Write down two ways that you can exhibit the selfless love of God toward others.

_____

_____

_____

Do you have on the shoes of the gospel of peace? (See Ephesians 6:15.) Are you prepared with the knowledge of the Word to tell others about Jesus? In the following lines, write a short paragraph of what you would say to tell someone about Jesus (Yeshua). You can use your Bible. Some clues can be found in John chapter 3, Romans chapters 3 and 6, and verses 9 and 10 of Romans chapter 10.

_____

_____

_____

_____

_____

_____

_____

The Word of God says in Jeremiah 31:3 that God has loved us with an everlasting love and with loving kindness He has drawn us. God loves us so much that even when we were still sinners Christ died for us (Rom. 5:8). On the following lines, write how much Jesus (Yeshua) loves *you*! Are there other scriptures that speak His love to you personally? Write them down also:

_____

_____

_____

_____

_____

_____

This chapter talks about the garden of the Lord, or you could call it the Garden of Eden, which is also within us. As Jesus, who is the perfect gardener, lives within us, He is all the while producing the fruit of God's character as listed in Galatians 5:22–23: Love, joy, peace, patience, kindness, goodness, faith, meekness, and self-control.

1. Are all these fruit being produced in your life?

_____

Which ones are being produced in your life? List them here:

_____

_____

_____

_____

Which ones are not being produced? List them here:

_____

_____

_____

Pray a prayer asking the Father to show you those areas that are not operating in your life and ask Him to work these areas into your life.

Read John 15:1–16. In the Word of God it says that even when you are producing fruit, God will prune all the dead limbs and that which is not producing. That which is dead and not producing takes away the life from that which is able to produce. When you go through trials, sometimes God is pruning the dead and unproductive areas of your life.

Can you recall a trial that when you look back you can see that God was pruning you? Write down that experience and what fruit was produced afterwards. If you are not sure, ask the Lord to show you what fruit was produced (patience, self-control, love your enemies, etc.).

_____

_____

_____

_____

_____

_____

Read Song of Solomon 5:2–9.

1. When the Lord calls you in the night, do you get up and spend time with Him? _____

THE SECRET PLACE TEACHING AND STUDY GUIDE

CHAPTER 11: THE THRONE ROOM

WHEN YOU GO through trials and you feel like you are being crushed or feel you are being beaten to a pulp (so to speak). I'm not talking physical or sexual abuse. I'm talking about trials that make you feel overwhelmed. Jesus said, "Be of good cheer, I have overcome the world." When this happens it means that New Wine and New Seed are being produced in you. The Father wants to pour out New Wine through you to others to strengthen and invigorate them. He also wants to pour out His Word through you to bring resurrection life into others.

As you spend more time with Yeshua He will take you deeper into Himself. He will make you one with Him as you continue to surrender to Him. Write down two ways you can personally surrender to the Lord Jesus (Yeshua):

1. _____

2. _____

3. _____

4. _____

There are three ways that you come into the throne room of God. You must have clean hands and a pure heart (Ps. 24:3–5) in confession and repentance first. Then access can come through prayer and also through thanksgiving and praise and worship (Ps. 100). Your prayers are like a sweet odor, a sacrifice to the Lord. Worship begins with thanksgiving and then moves into praise and finally worship. Psalm 100:4 says, "Enter into His gates with thanksgiving, And into His courts with praise." You come into the holy of holies through prayer and worship.

In thanksgiving

Tell God how thankful you are for what He has done. Sometimes you can thank Him before you see the answer to your prayers. Write below how thankful you are to Him.

_____

_____

_____

_____

In praise

Praise Him for His greatness and His power over all things. Write below something you can praise Him for:

_____

_____

_____

_____

In worship

Worship Him for who He is. This is a good time to proclaim to Him that He is the King of kings and Lord of lords and that His name is above every name and at the name of Jesus every knee will bow and every tongue confess that Jesus Christ is Lord (Phil. 2:9–11). Write below something that would express your personal worship toward God:

_____

_____

_____

_____

Now move on into deeper more intimate worship. He wants to bring you into the deeper intimacy of worship (you are His beloved and He is your Beloved). Put on soft worship music or sing love songs to Him out of your heart. Read the Song of Solomon out loud to Him. He responds to a heart that flows out with love for Him for just who He is because He is love and He loves you. Get all alone with Him and tell Him you want to lavish your love on Him. You can do like Mary did with the alabaster box of oil when she wept and kissed His feet and washed His feet with her tears. You may also kneel, bow, or dance before Him. Write below your experience:

_____

_____

_____

_____

Do you sense or feel a response from the Lord? Explain how you felt and what He said in His response to you. Be as detailed as possible.

_____

_____

_____

_____

Remember the Lord has delivered you from all your fears. The enemy will continue to test you to see if you can stand on the Word, especially to see if you believe God and the power of His Word to go forth as a sharp sword, to cut the enemy down. It may be dealing with fear, but there will also be testing in the areas of trust for healing and meeting of financial needs. Find scriptures or words to stand on. God has promised deliverance through His promises.

1. Fear and Faith): _____

2. Healing and Deliverance): _____

3. Finances and Provision): _____

God wants to bring us to a place of rest. That place is where we have such trust in God and His ability to provide that we can just say the Word and God brings the victory. Ask God to show you a weak area or areas in your faith. Now ask Him to show you a promise that will bring the victory.

Write the weakness or weaknesses.

_____

_____

_____

Write the promise scripture or scriptures.

_____

_____

_____

_____

THE SECRET PLACE TEACHING AND STUDY GUIDE

CHAPTER 12: HOLY GROUND AND HIGH PLACES

THIS CHAPTER HAS to do with understanding the eyes of your spirit and the Holy Spirit that dwells within you. The eyes of the spirit are in your inner imagination. It's like seeing pictures in your mind. Only these pictures or visual imaginations are from the Holy Spirit showing you the things of God in the spirit realm. This has to do with the prophetic realm. Sometimes God will use dreams as well to show us future things.

1. Have you ever had dreams and you know they came from God? _____

If you have, write the dream in the following lines. If you haven't then ask the Lord to give you dreams from Him.

_____

_____

_____

_____

2. Have you ever had an inner vision? _____

Write what you saw. If you haven't then ask the Lord to open your spiritual eyes (imagination) so you can see.

_____

_____

_____

3. Have you ever seen an open vision or an angel with your natural eyes? _____

If yes, write down what you saw.

_____

_____

_____

_____

You step on holy ground through prayer, praise and worship, and fasting. Holy ground also is a place to be spiritually and physically refreshed. A watchman is someone who prays and the Lord reveals His secrets and the future things to come. That's what dreams and visions from the Lord are for—for yourself and to give to others.

1. Has God ever given you a vision or a word for someone else? _____

2. What did He say to that person?

_____

_____

_____

God wants to help us and encourage us. He even wants to protect us. When we are sensitive to the Holy Spirit, our steps will be directed and He will keep us out of danger.

1. Has the Holy Spirit ever warned you about something? _____

2. What did He say?

_____

_____

_____

As watchmen we must be sensitive to the Holy Spirit's voice and unction. Has God given you a warning for someone else? Write down what He said.

_____

_____

_____

_____

THE SECRET PLACE TEACHING AND STUDY GUIDE

CHAPTER 13: STRONGHOLDS

REMEMBER A STRONGHOLD is a thinking pattern that is either a lie from the enemy Satan or a habit pattern, a belief that is contrary to the truth of the Word of God.

Make a list of strongholds (or habits) you are having trouble getting free from. Examples would be fear or untrue thoughts, such as, "I'm a sinner and there is no help for me," or "I'm not worth anything, or God doesn't love me," etc.).

_____

_____

_____

_____

Find scriptures in the Word of God that will counteract that stronghold. Yeshua will ride to you and bring His fiery truth and consume the lies of the enemy. Write these scriptures here.

_____

_____

_____

_____

The best news is that there is no condemnation for those who are in Christ Jesus, who walk not after the flesh, but after the Spirit. For the law of the Spirit of life in Christ Jesus has set you free from the law of sin and death (Rom. 8:1–2). (The enemy here is the demonic realm behind people.) The Lord will come to your aid. Fill in the blanks for these scriptures.

Psalm 18:13–14: "The Lord also _____ from the _____, and the Most High uttered His _____, amid hailstones and coals of fire. And He sent out His _____ and _____ them; and He flashed forth _____ and put them to _____" (AMPC).

Psalm 18:16–17: "He reached from on high, He took me; He _____ me out of many _____. He _____ me from my strong _____ and from those who hated and abhorred me, for they were too _____ for me" (AMPC).

Psalm 18:19: "He _____ me forth into a _____ place; He was _____ me because He was _____ with me and delighted in me" (AMPC).

Psalm 18:36–38: "You have given plenty of _____ for my _____ under me, that my feet would not slip. I _____ my enemies and _____ them; neither did I turn again till they were _____. I _____ them so that they were not able to _____; they fell _____ under my _____" (AMPC).

Psalm 18:39, 42–44: "For You have girded me with _____ for the battle; You have _____ under me and caused to _____ down those who _____ up against me.... Then I beat them _____ as the dust before the wind; I emptied them out as the _____ and mire of the streets. You have _____ me from the _____ of the people; You have made me the _____ of the nations; a people I had not known _____ me. As soon as they [demonic spirits] heard of me, they obeyed me; foreigners _____ themselves cringingly and _____ feigned obedience to me" (AMPC).

THE SECRET PLACE TEACHING AND STUDY GUIDE

CHAPTER 14: ON EAGLES WINGS

I N DEUTERONOMY 31:6 God said that "He will not fail you nor forsake you" (AMPC). Even if you have done something you are ashamed of, Jesus will never leave you and never forsake you. He loves you with the highest of all loves. Remember, Christ Jesus gave His life for you. God is not fickle in His character, He always keeps His Word. When you go through a trial, stretch out your hand and hold on to Him and His Word (promises). He will bring you through to victory.

Is there some area of your life that you are having difficulty with? Write it down below and give it to Him.

_____

_____

_____

_____

Now find some scriptures that relate to that situation. Write them below.

_____

_____

_____

_____

Speak and declare those scriptures out loud over yourself. Meditate on God's saving power spoken of in these scriptures. It may take days before you see a change, so don't be discouraged or give up. The Spirit of God and the angels are coming to your rescue. God is keeping you. He is raising you up and carrying you on His mighty wings to victory.

Read and meditate on Psalm 91 and God will deliver you from all your fears.

As we go through the trials and the tribulations, the strength of the Lord will give you grace to overcome. We are in what is called a spiritual boot camp for the Lord. The Holy Spirit is training us to be fearless mighty warriors for Him. As we lean on our beloved Yeshua and trust in Him, He will bring us the victory.

Write a letter of thanksgiving or a love letter to the Lord expressing your love and thankfulness.

_____

_____

_____

_____

_____

THE SECRET PLACE TEACHING AND STUDY GUIDE

Chapter 15: Eye of the Eagle

As you move closer to the Lord, He will open your spiritual eyes more to spiritual things. Sometimes He will open your eyes to principalities and powers, but that is not what we are to dwell on. Our eyes should be on the Lord of Hosts, Jehovah Sabaoth, who is our Lord and leader in this great battle of the end of the age. We must seek His face and seek God's wisdom for winning this battle.

One of the greatest weapons is God's love for us and flowing through us. In 2 Corinthians 10:3–4 it says, "For though we walk in the flesh, we do not war according to the flesh. For the weapons of our warfare are not carnal but mighty in God for pulling down strongholds." God is saying that His weapons are not what we would normally think of as weapons in the natural. He wants us to use the Word of God as our weapon, the fruit of the Spirit (motivated by love), which is God's holy character, and prayer, praise, and worship.

We must seek the Lord for strategy to come against our enemy Satan. Jesus gave examples of how God got the victory through simple ordinary people. He even was able to use a person who didn't think he was usable by God because of the flaws he saw in himself. But God only saw the greatness. Most of the people God used were hidden away until God brought them out. Examples would be Moses, Joshua, Gideon, Esther, and so many more.

God sees greatness in you and He calls it forth in you every day. Remember, Jesus is daily making intercession for you (Heb. 7:25) and calling those things that seem not as though they were (Rom. 4:17). God said, "'Let there be light'; and there was light" (Gen. 1:3). He called for light to dispel the darkness.

David asked the Lord for wisdom concerning a battle and God gave David wisdom but it was God who won the victory (see

2 Samuel 5:19–25). One of the most powerful weapons is praise. The story of Paul and Silas is a great example. They were in prison; but when they began to praise the Lord, that which had kept them imprisoned and in bondage trembled and quaked and the foundations of that demonic stronghold was shaken to the core and the prison doors were opened (see Acts 16:16–31).

Second Samuel, chapter 22, beginning in verse 2 and ending with verse 4, says,

> The LORD is my rock and my fortress and my deliverer; the God of my strength, in whom will I trust; My shield and the horn [strength] of my salvation, My stronghold and my refuge; My Savior, you save me from violence. I will call on the LORD, who is worthy to be praised; So shall I be saved from my enemies.

This is because the Lord is our high tower, our safety. God's protection and ability to protect is greater than Satan's power to imprison.

Is there an area in your life where you feel imprisoned? Write that situation below and then either use the psalm above or a similar scripture to praise and worship the Lord so He can send His angels to free you (either a prison mindset or emotional prison).

_____

_____

_____

_____

Write any other scriptures here.

_____

_____

_____

_____

Enter His gates with thanksgiving And His courts with praise. Give thanks to Him, bless His name. For the LORD is good; His lovingkindness is everlasting And His faithfulness to all generations.

—PSALM 100:4–5, NAS

Sing for joy in the LORD, O you righteous ones, praise is becoming to the upright. Give thanks to the LORD with the lyre; sing praises to Him with a harp of ten strings. Sing to Him a new song; Play skillfully with a shout of joy.

—PSALM 33:1–3, NAS

You may not have a harp or lyre, but you can use a tambourine; or you have hands that can clap and a voice that can sing and shout. You can be set free just by praising God. God is no respecter of persons (Rom. 2:11). He looks at the heart (1 Sam. 16:7), and He doesn't judge whether the voice is melodically correct or not. Just abandon yourself to the Lord and lift up a sound to Him with love in your heart. You will be liberated.

THE SECRET PLACE TEACHING AND STUDY GUIDE

CHAPTER 16: HEAVENLY WARRIOR

P RAY TO THE Lord and cry out for spiritual discernment as it
says in Isaiah 11:2–3,

> The Spirit of the LORD will rest upon Him, The Spirit
> of wisdom and understanding, the Spirit of counsel and
> might, the Spirit of knowledge and of the fear of the LORD.
> His delight is in the fear of the LORD, And He shall not
> judge by the sight of His eyes, Nor decide by the hearing
> of His ears.

This same Holy Spirit rests upon us and has imparted these same
anointings on us, and they dwell in us because of Jesus. Ask the
Lord to open your spiritual ears to hear the Spirit's wisdom, counsel,
and knowledge and to open your spiritual eyes to see things, people,
and situations as they truly are. With your spiritual eyes and ears
open, Satan will have a difficult time deceiving you no matter who
or what he sends against you.

We as believers must be watchmen on the wall in prayer, bringing
God's Word to His remembrance. Fill in the blanks for this scripture, Isaiah 62:6–7:

> I have set _____ on your walls, O Jerusalem; They shall
> never hold their _____ day or _____. You who make
> mention of the _____, do not keep _____, And
> give _____ no rest till He _____ And till He makes
> Jerusalem a _____ in the earth.

When we are praying, as believers, we are joining with our Lord,
as He is our leader, chief intercessor, and heavenly warrior. Please
fill in the blanks for these scriptures:

Romans 8:34: "Who is he who condemns? It is _____ who _____, and furthermore is also _____, who is even at the right _____ of God, who also makes _____ for us."

Hebrews 7:25: "Therefore He is also able to _____ to the uttermost those who come to God through Him, since He always lives to make _____ for them."

Join with Jesus in prayer because He is the Mighty One who has defeated Satan and made an open show of him. Please fill in the blanks for these scriptures:

Psalm 24:7–10: "Lift up your _____, O you _____! And be lifted up, you _____ doors! And the _____ of _____ shall come in. Who is this King of _____? The LORD _____ and _____, the LORD mighty in _____. Lift up your _____, O you _____! Lift up, you _____ doors! And the _____ of glory shall come in. Who is this King of glory? The LORD of _____ [Jehovah Sabaoth], He is the King of _____."

Colossians 2:13–15: "And you, being dead in your _____ and the _____ of your flesh, He has made _____ together with Him, having _____ you all _____, having wiped out the _____ of _____ that was _____ us. And He has _____ it out of the _____, having _____ it to the _____. Having disarmed _____ and _____, He made a _____ spectacle of them, _____ over them in it [the cross]."

THE SECRET PLACE TEACHING AND STUDY GUIDE

CHAPTER 17: THE FINAL BATTLE

BEFORE GOING INTO prayer, make sure that you put on the whole armor of God and cover yourself in the blood of Jesus. Please fill in the blanks for this scripture:

> Stand firm then, with the belt of _____ buckled around
> your waist, with the _____ of _____ in place, and
> with your _____ fitted with the _____ readiness
> that comes from the gospel of _____. In addition to all
> this, take up the shield of _____, with which you can
> _____ all the _____ arrows of the evil one. Take the
> helmet of _____ and the _____ of the Spirit, which
> is the _____.
>
> —EPHESIANS 6:14–17, NIV

We are to keep awake in spirit and in prayer. Fill in the blanks for these scriptures:

1 Peter 5:8: "Be sober, be _____; because your adversary the _____ walks about as a roaring _____, seeking whom he may _____."

James 4:7: "Therefore submit to God. _____ the devil and he will _____ from you.

Are you ready for the Lord's return? Read Matthew 25:1–13 and learn from this scripture to be filled with the Holy Spirit at all times. Please fill in the blanks for Matthew 25:6–13.

> And at _____ a cry was heard: "Behold, the _____
> is coming; go out to meet him!" Then all those _____
> arose and _____ their lamps. And the _____
> said to the wise, "Give us some of your _____, for

our _____ are going _____." But the _____
answered, saying, "_____, lest there should _____
be enough for us and you; but _____ rather to those
who _____, and _____ for yourselves." And while
they went to _____, the _____ came, and those
who were _____ went in with him to the _____;
and the _____ was shut. Afterward the _____
virgins came also, saying, "Lord, Lord, _____ to us!"
But he answered and said, "Assuredly, I say to you, I
_____ know you." _____ therefore, for you
know neither the _____ nor the _____ in which the
_____ of _____ is coming.

There were five wise virgins and five foolish. The five wise virgins had a personal intimate relationship with the Lord and the
Holy Spirit. Because of that intimacy with the Lord, the Lord Jesus
Christ *knew* them because that they were always being filled with
the Holy Spirit.

Ephesians 3:16–19 in the New Living Translation says:

> I pray that from his glorious, unlimited resources he will
> empower you with inner strength through his Spirit. Then
> Christ will make his home in your hearts as you trust in
> him. Your roots will grow down into God's love and keep
> you strong. And may you have the power to understand,
> as all God's people should, how wide, how long, how high,
> and how deep his love is. May you experience the love of
> Christ, though it is too great to understand fully. Then
> you will be made complete with all the fullness of life and
> power that comes from God.

Ephesians 3:19 in the Amplified Bible says:

> [That you may really come] to know [practically, through
> experience for yourselves] the love of Christ, which far sur-
> passes mere knowledge [without experience]; that you may
> be filled [through all your being] unto all the fullness of
> God [may have the richest measure of the divine Presence,

and become a body wholly filled and flooded with God
Himself]!

These scriptures tell us that love and intimacy with the Lord
Jesus Christ is of utmost importance.

THE SECRET PLACE TEACHING AND STUDY GUIDE

CHAPTER 18: THE BRIDE

Remember, any of the hard things you are going through, if you are a believer in Jesus (Yeshua), are only to prepare you to rule and reign. Just as Yeshua learned obedience by the things He suffered, so must we. Just like Esther in the Book of Esther was washed and cleansed for six months in oil of myrrh and six months in sweet spices and perfumes for purifying, so must we go through purifying before we meet our King Yeshua. The main thing that must be cleansed from us is pride or haughtiness. The Lord will humble us in many areas and many ways. Fill in the blanks for these scriptures.

Proverbs 16:18: "_____ goes before destruction, And a _____ spirit before a fall."

1 Peter 5:5: "God _____ the _____, But gives _____ to the _____."

Proverbs 29:23: "A man's _____ will bring him _____, But the _____ in spirit will retain _____."

Obadiah 1:3: "The _____ of your heart has _____ you, You who dwell in the clefts of the rock, Whose habitation is high; You who say in your heart, 'Who will bring me _____ to the ground?'"

Matthew 23:12: "And whoever _____ himself will be _____, and he who _____ himself will be _____."

Read Luke 7:36–50. Even when we sin God will forgive us. Please fill in the blanks for Luke 7:44–48, 50.

Then He [Yeshua] turned to the woman and said to Simon, "Do you see this woman? I entered your house; you gave

Me no _____ for My _____, but she has _____
My _____ with her _____ and _____ them with
the _____ of her _____. You gave Me no _____,
but this _____ has not _____ to _____ My
_____ since the time I came in. You did not _____
My head with _____, but this woman has _____
My _____ with fragrant _____. Therefore I say to
you, her _____, which are _____, are _____, for
she _____ much. But to whom _____ is _____,
the same _____." Then He said to her, "Your
_____ are _____."…Then He said to the woman,
"Your _____ has _____ you. Go in _____."

Out of thanksgiving to God for saving you and keeping you for
such a time as this, write a love letter, poem, or song to the Lord in
gratitude for what He has done for you.

_____

_____

_____

_____

_____

_____

THE SECRET PLACE TEACHING AND STUDY GUIDE

Chapter 19: The Marriage Supper

HAVE WE ALLOWED ourselves to be washed by the water of the Word of God? Fill in the blanks for this scripture in Ephesians 5:25–27.

> Husbands, _____ your wives, as Christ also _____ the _____ and gave Himself for her, that He might _____ and _____ her with the _____ of water by the _____, that He might _____ her to Himself a glorious church, not having _____ or _____ or any such thing, but that she should be _____ and without _____.

Verse 27 speaks of Christ cleansing us and getting us prepared. See the Book of Esther 2:12 to see how we are being washed and purified by the Word and the Holy Spirit.

Fill in the blanks for Revelation 3:18.

> I counsel you to buy from Me _____ refined in the _____, that you may be rich, and _____ that you may be clothed, that the shame of your nakedness may not be _____; and anoint your _____ with eye salve, that you may see.

Our part to be prepared to be Christ's bride and for the wedding supper of the Lamb is to spend time with the Lord and in His Word and to seek first the kingdom of God that is in Yeshua the Messiah.

Another thing we are responsible for is to bring others into the kingdom so they too can take part in the marriage supper of the Lamb. Not only are we to tell others about Jesus, but we are to help the Lord disciple the new babes coming in.

Read Jesus' parable on the wedding banquet in Matthew 22:1–14.
Some of those who were invited didn't come, so

> Those servants went out on the crossroads and got together
> as many as they found, both bad and good, so the [room
> in which] wedding feast [was held] was filled with guests.
> But when the king came in to view the guests, he looked
> intently at a man there who had on no wedding garment.
> And he said, Friend, how did you come in here without
> putting on the [appropriate] wedding garment? And he
> was speechless (muzzled, gagged). Then the king said to
> the attendants, Tie him hand and foot, and throw him into
> the darkness outside; there will be weeping and grinding
> of teeth, for many are called (invited and summoned), but
> few are chosen.
>
> —MATTHEW 22:10–14, AMPC

THE SECRET PLACE TEACHING AND STUDY GUIDE

CHAPTER 20: THE WEDDING

ARE WE READY for the wedding of the Lamb? Fill in the blanks for this scripture in Revelation 19:7–8.

Let us be glad and _____ and give Him _____, for the _____ of the _____ has come, and His _____ has made herself _____. And to her it was granted to be _____ in fine _____, clean and _____, for the fine linen is the _____ acts of the saints.

As you draw closer to the Lord you will desire more of Yeshua and less of the world. Your desire will be to minister to and for the Lord. As He draws you to Himself, He will continue to say, "Arise My love and come away with Me!" In these last days He will call us more and more to come with Him into the fields of harvest to bring others into the kingdom to tell others about our Bridegroom so they can become part of the bride.

As the Lord draws you, you will desire a life of holiness, conse-crated and set apart for God's holy use. You will hunger and thirst more for the righteousness of God which is in Christ Jesus (2 Cor. 5:21). Fill in the blanks for these scriptures:

Matthew 5:6: "Blessed are those who _____ and thirst for _____, For they shall be _____."

Psalm 4:3: "But know that the LORD has _____ apart for Himself him who is _____; The LORD will _____ when I call to Him."

Colossians 3:1–3: "If then you were raised with Christ, _____ those things which are _____, where Christ is, _____ at the right hand of God. Set your _____ on things _____, not on things on the _____. For you _____, and your life is _____ with Christ in God."

Exodus 19:10–11: "And the LORD said to Moses, "Go to the _____ and _____ them today and tomorrow, and let them _____ their clothes. And let them be _____ for the _____ day. For on the third day the _____ will come down upon Mount Sinai in the _____ of all the people."

John 17:16–19: "They are not of the _____, just as I am not of the world. _____ them by Your truth. Your _____ is truth. As you sent Me into the world, I also have sent them into the _____. And for their sakes I _____ Myself, that they also may be sanctified by the _____.

THE SECRET PLACE TEACHING AND STUDY GUIDE

CHAPTER 21: THE BRIDAL CHAMBER

HAVE YOU COME to the place of total surrender to the Lord? John the Baptist said in John 3:30, "He [Jesus] must increase, but I must decrease."

Yeshua (Jesus) was sent by the Father to the earth to become the new Adam. In Genesis 2:21–24 we read where the Lord God caused a deep sleep to fall upon the first Adam; and while he slept, the Lord took one of his ribs or a part of his side and closed up the place with flesh. And the rib or part of his side which the Lord God had taken from the man He made into a woman, and He brought her to the man. Then Adam said, "This is now bone of my bones, And flesh of my flesh; She shall be called Woman, Because she was taken out of a man" (v. 23). Verse 24 then says, "Therefore a man shall leave his father and mother and shall become united and cleave to his wife, and they shall become one flesh" (AMPC).

The same idea was exhibited in Jesus (Yeshua), who is the new Adam; for the Lord caused the deep sleep of death to come upon Jesus. On the day He was crucified, the bride of Christ Jesus came forth from His side when blood and water came forth as His side was pierced. John 19:34 says, "But one of the soldiers pierced His side with a spear, and immediately blood and water came [flowed] out." When a baby is born, blood and water come out with the baby. Therefore I believe Jesus' (Yeshua's) bride was taken out of His side as the blood and water came out and the church (the bride) was birthed. Now the new Adam, Christ, says of the bride, "She is now bone of my bone and flesh of my flesh; she shall be called the church, because she was taken out of My side."

In Ephesians, chapter 1, it says that we are the church and the body of Christ. Verses 22 and 23 say, "And He has put all things under His feet and has appointed Him the universal and supreme Head of the church [a headship exercised throughout the church],

Which is His body the fullness of Him Who fills all in all [for in that body lives the full measure of Him Who makes everything complete, and Who fills everything everywhere with Himself]" (AMPC).

Therefore, we are His body here on this earth to be His hands, feet, eyes, and mouth to the whole world. Every day we should look for His coming that we may spend eternity with Him. When we are resurrected with Him, either in the Rapture or in death, we will no longer have this body of flesh to separate us from Him and we will be free to experience the greatness of His love for us.

As it says in Ephesians 3,

> [We will] . . . have the power and be strong to apprehend and grasp with all the saints God's devoted people, the experience of that love] what is the breadth and length and height and depth [of it]. [That you may really come] to know [practically, through experience for yourselves] the love of Christ, which far surpasses mere knowledge [without experience]; that you may be filled [through all your being] unto all the fullness of God [may have the richest measure of the divine Presence, and become a body wholly filled and flooded with God Himself]!
>
> —EPHESIANS 3:18–19, AMPC

We don't know what it will be like when we are raptured and are with Him in the bridal chamber during the seven years of the tribulation that will be on the earth. But we know there will be such love that at this time we are unable to comprehend.

Read Psalm 45 and fill in the blanks for Psalm 45:6–11, 13–15.

> Your _____, O God, is _____ and ever; A _____ of _____ is the _____ of Your kingdom. You love _____ and _____ wickedness; Therefore _____, Your God, has _____ You with the _____ of gladness above Your _____. All Your _____ are scented with _____ and aloes and _____, Out of the _____ palaces, by which they have _____ You _____. Kings' daughters are among Your _____ women; At Your _____ hand stands the _____ in _____ from

Ophir. Listen, O daughter, Consider and incline your ear;
_____ your own people also, and your _____ house;
So the _____ will greatly _____ your _____;
Because He is your _____, worship Him.... The royal
_____ is all _____ within the palace; Her clothing is
woven with _____. She shall be _____ to the King
in _____ of many colors; The _____, her _____
who follow her, shall be _____ to You. With _____
and _____ they shall be _____; They shall _____
the King's _____.

THE SECRET PLACE TEACHING AND STUDY GUIDE

LOOK UP THIS scripture and fill in the blanks.

Matthew 6:10, 13b: "Your _____ come, Your _____ be _____ On earth as it is in heaven....For Yours is the _____ and the _____ and the _____ forever. Amen.

This is a prayer for God's kingdom to live in man. Yeshua carried God's kingdom within Himself; and through His death, burial, and resurrection, He imparted that kingdom into us who believe. But when Yeshua comes to earth and finally puts to naught the works of Satan, then the fullness of the kingdom will come. We are now only sampling a foretaste of what is to come.

The kingdom of God shall look like this. Fill in the blanks.

That our _____ may be as _____ grown up in their _____; That our _____ may be as pillars, _____ in palace style; That our _____ may be full, Supplying all kinds of _____; That our _____ may bring forth _____ And ten _____ in our fields; That our _____ may be _____; that there be no _____ in, nor _____ out; That there be no _____ in our streets. _____ are the people who are in such a state; Happy are the people whose _____ is the _____!

—PSALM 144:12–15

Fill in the blanks for Revelation 21:1–4.

Now I saw a _____ heaven and a new _____, for the _____ heaven and the first _____ had _____ away. Also there was no more _____. Then I, _____, saw the _____ city, New _____, coming down out of _____ from God, prepared as a _____ adorned for her _____. And I _____ a loud _____ from _____ saying, "Behold, the _____ of God is with _____, and He will _____ with them, and they shall be His _____. _____ Himself will be with them and be their _____. And _____ shall wipe away every _____ from their _____; there shall be no more _____, nor _____, nor _____. There shall be no more _____, for the _____ things have _____ away."

THE SECRET PLACE TEACHING AND STUDY GUIDE

CHAPTER 23: YESHUA THE KING

THIS CHAPTER IS Yeshua's final word to the church and to the world. Revelation 3:18 says,

> I counsel you to buy from Me gold refined in the fire, that you may be rich, and white garments, that you may be clothed, that the shame of your nakedness may not be revealed; and anoint your eyes with eye salve, that you may see.

The gold here represents the work of the Holy Spirit to purify you through the Word and through the trying of your faith which can be like fire burning up the dross (1 Pet. 1:7). White raiment is the washing of the water of the Word as well as being obedient to the voice of God and doing the deeds He asked you to do. Anointing eyes with eye salve represents the Word of truth so that you will no longer be spiritually blind.

The Lord is making a plea to repent and turn to Him because the time is drawing near for the door of grace will soon be closing.

> Repent therefore and be converted, that your sins may be blotted out, so that times of refreshing may come from the presence of the Lord, and that He may send Jesus Christ....
> —ACTS 3:19–20

ABOUT THE AUTHOR

Constance (Connie) is a native of Oklahoma. She was born in Oklahoma City and grew up in Tulsa where she met her husband. She attended Central State College now known as University of Central Oklahoma. She and her husband were transferred to Houston area with an oil company and settled in Missouri City, Texas, where they now reside. She is a member of the Freedom Center Church where she volunteers and also teaches a Bible study to several ladies. She and her husband have two grown sons and a daughter-in-law who reside in the south Houston area.

CONTACT THE AUTHOR

Website:
www.gardengatewayinternational.com

E-mail address:
connie1.4@juno.com

Mailing address:
P.O. Box 1215,
Missouri City,
Texas 77459-1215

If you have asked Yeshua (Jesus, Isa) into your heart because of this book, please let the author know by emailing her at connie1.4@ juno.com.